SO YOU FEEL LIKE GOD'S NOT THERE?

The hiding of God and how you can find Him

Robert J Emery

Copyright © 2020 Robert J Emery

All rights reserved

The rights of Robert J Emery to be identified as the author of this work has been asserted by him per the Copyright, Designs and Patents Act 1988.

All rights reserved. No part of this publication may be reproduced or transmitted in any form or by any means electronic or mechanical, including photocopy, recording or any information storage and retrieval system, without permission in writing from the author.

Scripture taken from the NEW AMERICAN STANDARD BIBLE, © Copyright The Lockman Foundation 1960, 1962, 1963, 1968, 1971, 1972, 1973, 1975, 1977, 1988, 1995. Used by permission.

Please note that satan is not capitalised, even though it is a noun and that English grammar requires it to be capitalised. At the expense of grammar, I choose not to recognise him.

ISBN 9798695767391

Cover design: https://pxhere.com/en/photo/937214
Prined by Amazon

If you are experiencing confusion, pain, and suffering, it may be that God is working things out for you in his own way. It is most often the sovereign work of our God unfolding a master plan known only to him.

- DAVID WILKERSON

CONTENTS

Title Page	1
Copyright	2
Epigraph	3
Preface	7
Acknowledgements	11
Chapter One: A word for the seeker	13
Chapter Two: What is Truth?	17
Chapter Three: Seeking Him	24
Chapter Four: To Obey	31
Chapter Five: Reconciliation with Others	39
Chapter Six: Unforgiveness	45
Chapter Seven: Rebellion	52
Chapter Eight: Pride, the Christian's enemy	59
Chapter Nine: Besetting Sin	67
Chapter Ten: Love the Bride	81
Chapter Eleven: Getting over the 'Crowd Effect'	86
Chapter Twelve: Suffering	93
Chapter Thirteen: Spiritual depression	106
Chapter Fourteen: When God hides His Face	115
Chapter Fifteen: The Intellectual's Barrier	122
References	127

PREFACE

I began writing this book in 2014 after I had read a poem online:

> *"And where is God when I'm crying,*
> *Sobbing because I am broken?*
> *And why doesn't he speak to me?"* [1]

Reading this beautiful poem, it suddenly struck me that many times we feel alone as Christians while God seems to be far away from us. I have spent two years studying at Bible College from 2015 – 2017 and another two years after that volunteering at the same College.

I learnt many things in this place, yet it was not here that this publication was birthed, but instead, it came out of my own experiences in the wilderness. A dry, empty desert while God was teaching me about Himself and the areas in my life that were creating the blockages between me and the fullness of a close relationship with Him that I had been praying for. The result, of course, is what is before you now.

Don't suppose that I come from some higher place than you to impose on you what I think is right. When I first became a believer by committing my life fully to Jesus Christ, I went through a tough time. My family and I would go to Church. There would always be one of them who would exclaim, "Wow! The presence of God was awesome during worship!" However, I would never feel a thing. We would decide to pray together and behold, expressions of thankfulness to God's closeness would ensue. Despite being serious in my faith, God never touched me during these times. I began feeling very upset, that maybe there was something very evil in me that God had to keep His distance away from. But He spoke to me:

"I want you to seek Me with all of your heart until you find Me."

I started praying every day for hours at a time, and I devoured the Bible. Because I sought Him and didn't give up the pursuit, I found Him at last. In fact, many godly men and women in the Bible felt the same way that you may now feel.

Arouse Yourself, why do You sleep, O Lord?
Awake, do not reject us forever.
Why do You hide Your face
And forget our affliction and our oppression?
- Psalm 44:23-24

It may seem like God is ignoring you, despite all you do for Him. However, please note it is not really about what you do for God. He is looking for you, not what you can do for Him. God delights in being found by us more than we delight in finding Him. We must not give up on God because He feels distant. We must continue to seek Him until He is found.

Seek the Lord while He may be found;
Call upon Him while He is near.
- Isaiah 55:6

Do not give up. Do not turn to other gods as other people have done. Truly I tell you that He is the one true God. Seek Him and allow Him to work in your life. Everything He does in your life is all designed to bring you closer to Himself. Believe that and accept that my friends. He loves you. If I can leave you with one verse that would sum up the totality of this book it would be this:

Who is among you who fears the Lord,
Who obeys the voice of His servant,
Who walks in darkness and has no light?
Let him trust in the name of the Lord and rely on his God.
- Isaiah 50:10

At the end of every chapter is a prayer you can pray which is related to the topic addressed. The words are only a guideline. They must be your words, and they must come from your heart. God bless you with an encounter with the living Christ. The only Lord and Potentate!

ACKNOWLEDGEMENTS

When I read books, it is fascinating for me to see how many people the author thanks for their contributions. I never understood until I wrote my own just how much help and advice are needed for such a task. This publication was not only my work but with the thoughtful advice; thought-provoking comments and encouragements from many dear friends who took what I believed to be a good book and they helped to make it great. Without their valuable input, this book would not be what it now is. Amongst those are Frank Cook, Paul Hodgson and Paul Jackson whom I thank for commenting on the content of the book. Thank you to Grace Isaiah, my dear friend, for reading through the manuscript with thoughts and help with grammar. I cannot forget my parents for the godly upbringing I received as a child for these undoubtedly impacted me for good. Also a quick thank you is much needed, to Theo Onumah for being a good friend and encouraging my writing. Thank you also to Toby Robinson and Jerrin Glady for being the testers for this book and for giving me your thoughts accordingly. I also want to thank Matthew Hastings for his constructive advice on both the content of this book but also on the way in formatting it. Of course, above all, I want to extend my thanks to my loving Saviour Jesus Christ, who taught me that seeking Him is all my joy and my peace. To His Name be the honour and praise both now and forever. I love you, Jesus.

CHAPTER ONE: A WORD FOR THE SEEKER

All that the Father gives Me will come to Me, and the one who comes to Me I will certainly not cast out.

John 6:37

If you are desperate to know who God is and you really are looking for Him, you are actually in a very significant place. He loves you very much and wants a relationship with you, but there are some issues at hand that need to be addressed.

It could be asked why out of all the religions of the world is Christianity any different? It has been said a few times that religion is man's attempt to reach God, but Christianity is about God reaching down to men and women through His Son Jesus Christ. You must understand that God Himself came down as a Man and lived among humans. Human beings are made in the image of God, and this same God lowered Himself to become like a human.

Have this attitude in yourselves which was also in Christ Jesus,

> who, although He existed in the form of God, did not regard equality with God a thing to be grasped, but emptied Himself, taking the form of a bond-servant, and being made in the likeness of men. Being found in appearance as a man, He humbled Himself by becoming obedient to the point of death, even death on a cross.
>
> *- Philippians 2:5-8*

When you understand that God Himself took your sins upon Himself and died for you so that the punishment for all your sin and wrong-doing could be turned away from you, then you have grasped the reason why for hundreds of years millions of people gave their very lives to follow Jesus Christ.

Unfortunately, sometimes, Christians have been bad examples. They are, however, not perfect. Do not judge a perfect God by the way imperfect people behave. Jesus Christ is the best example of how a person should live as a Christian.

The Bible clearly teaches that there is a day of reckoning coming, a day of judgement in which God will judge the whole world in perfect righteousness. God will be totally and utterly fair. He hates sin so much he must judge it. No matter how big or small. He will deal with all sin and all wickedness – whether words, thoughts or deeds. And for all people without exception, this is awful news.

> who believes in the Son has eternal life; but he who does not obey the Son will not see life, but the wrath of God abides on him."
>
> *- John 3:36*

The situation is, but He loves the world, so He sends His warnings to people so that they may get out of trouble with God and become friends with God. This is His intention.

> Yet I sent you all My servants the prophets, again and again, saying, "Oh, do not do this abominable thing which I hate."
>
> *- Jeremiah 44:4*

The Lord is not slow about His promise, as some count slowness, but is patient toward you, not wishing for any to perish but for all to come to repentance.

- 2 Peter 3:9

God does not want anyone to go to hell, yet the truth is that God is so holy that no sin can go unpunished. 2000 years ago, God prepared a sacrifice. You are standing in the courtroom before a judge, and you are guilty of lying, stealing, looking at people with lustful intent (adultery of the heart) and misusing the Judge's Name (blasphemy) as a curse word. Jesus, at that moment, enters the courtroom and pays your fine for you (by dying on the cross and rising from the dead), so you don't have to go to prison (hell). All you have to do is turn away from your sinful lifestyle and put your faith entirely in Jesus Christ.

You cannot earn heaven by your good deeds. If somebody lends you a million pounds, of which you do not pay anything back and after he gives you more money than you do payback. The fact remains that you still owe one million pounds. Unless that past debt is clear, you will not be able to get rid of it by being kind and worse even you may get into a great deal of trouble over it. Only someone rich enough to pay those million pounds can help you. Jesus is willing to pay your debt to God if you would let Him.

For all of us have become like one who is unclean,
And all our righteous deeds are like a filthy garment;
And all of us wither like a leaf,
And our iniquities, like the wind, take us away.

- Isaiah 64:6

For by grace you have been saved through faith; and that not of yourselves, it is the gift of God; not as a result of works, so that no one may boast.

- Ephesians 2:8-9

You must come to God only through faith and only through the Lord Jesus Christ.

"For God so loved the world, that He gave His only begotten Son, that whoever believes in Him shall not perish, but have eternal life.

- John 3:16

Make the decision to follow Jesus Christ. He has not let down a single person who has trusted in Him.

To pray:

Father, I want to ask You to forgive my sin. I put all my trust in Jesus Christ, in His death on the cross and resurrection from the dead that it was entirely enough to pay off my debt of sin and make peace with You. I renounce my sin and evil choices. I choose to follow You. I only ask that the wall between us be separated. Come, Lord, I invite You to be the Lord and Master of my life. In Jesus' Name. Amen.

CHAPTER TWO: WHAT IS TRUTH?

And you will know the truth, and the truth will make you free.

John 8:32

One of the problems with this age (and this has been an ongoing problem since the birth of the Church) is that many people claim to have a relationship with Jesus Christ, but in actual reality, they don't really belong to Him. They look religious, they have a form of something that appears to have an association with God, but they deny the place where knowing the Lord is really supposed to lead them.

There are, in reality, many different Jesus'. There is a Jesus believed in by Mormons, a different Jesus by the Jehovah's Witnesses, and even in Islam, there is a belief in a man called Jesus. Each of these has a relationship with Jesus and many other religions and cults besides them. Yet which Jesus is actually the real Jesus? It's a serious question.

> *Not everyone who says to Me, 'Lord, Lord,' will enter the kingdom of heaven."*
>
> *- Matthew 7:21*

In Jesus Christ, God revealed himself to the world. He came to the earth to show us the way to God. But there is another person who always enters the scene as well as he did in the Garden of Eden at the beginning. That, of course, is the devil.

> *Jesus presented another parable to them, saying, "The kingdom of heaven may be compared to a man who sowed good seed in his field. But while his men were sleeping, his enemy came and sowed tares among the wheat, and went away. But when the wheat sprouted and bore grain, then the tares became evident also.*
>
> *- Matthew 13:24-26*

The good seed is divine truth that comes from God - the devil comes along also and sows his counterfeits and his lies. This is done to create confusion and chaos so that nobody can distinguish truth from error so that people might not discover the real truth that comes from God.

Think about it.

Why are there so many different religions in the world? Why are there different people saying different things about Jesus? How can one decipher what is right and what is not? When a man comes to God and puts his faith in His Son Jesus Christ, He gives this man His Holy Spirit to live inside his body with him (*John 14:16-18*).

> *But when He, the Spirit of truth, comes, He will guide you into all the truth; for He will not speak on His own initiative, but whatever He hears, He will speak; and He will disclose to you what is to come.*
>
> *- John 16:13*

So He is the Spirit of truth, what therefore is false is contrary to His nature.

> *And He, when He comes, will convict the world concerning sin*

and righteousness and judgment.
- John 16:8

When the Spirit of God comes, He will sound loud alarms when you sin. Even when you so much as start to think about sinning against God He will convict you for it. He will also put into your heart a desire to please God and live a life that is righteous before Him. More than that, He will bring to heart the coming judgement, that you will be reminded that your focus and your attention is not for this world but for that which is to come.

But we all, with unveiled face, beholding as in a mirror the glory of the Lord, are being transformed into the same image from glory to glory, just as from the Lord, the Spirit.
- 2 Corinthians 3:18

Is there a change taking place in your heart? However little or slowly it is, are you becoming more like Jesus? If you are precisely the same person you are as you were before you 'accepted Christ,' that being: in your conduct, where you go, what you do, what you say and what you think, then it is very alarming and concerning, to say the least. It does admittedly take time to change, but if you haven't changed at all and are still carrying on in the practices that God speaks against with no thought of it, then you are still living in sin. You may be religious and even be an active Church member, but it is not these things that you do which save you. It's all about being born again when He comes to live in your heart and changes you. The religious acts of themselves are meaningless.

The one who says, "I have come to know Him," and does not keep His commandments, is a liar, and the truth is not in him.
- 1 John 2:4

You cannot have a deep and significant relationship with God and continue a relationship with sin. When one is at peace with God, it also follows that he has made war against his sin. The danger is to justify wrong and try to have peace with God at the same time. Yet the standards that God requires His people to live by are high.

> *And He said to them, "You are those who justify yourselves in the sight of men, but God knows your hearts; for that which is highly esteemed among men is detestable in the sight of God.*
>
> *- Luke 16:15*

God requires honesty. He knows the truth anyway but appreciates it when a man speaks to Him in transparency.

> *The Lord is near to all who call upon Him, to all who call upon Him in truth.*
>
> *- Psalm 145:18*

Now, remember that everything the Spirit says will always be in complete harmony with the Bible – **always**. The Bible must be accepted to be totally infallible and free from error.

> *All Scripture is inspired by God and profitable for teaching, for reproof, for correction, for training in righteousness; so that the man of God may be adequate, equipped for every good work.*
>
> *- 2 Timothy 3:16-17*

The Bible is the sole source of what God is saying to us. God still speaks directly, but He has given to mankind the Bible to be the standard of ultimate truth. The Bible is always relevant, no matter what the world says. Everything that doesn't match up to what is in the Bible **must** be rejected. No matter how loving, kind, pure or noble, they claim or appear to be. All other things come from satan himself.

> *But even if we, or an angel from heaven, should preach to you a gospel contrary to what we have preached to you, he is to be accursed! As we have said before, so I say again now, if any man is preaching to you a gospel contrary to what you received, he is to be accursed!*

- Galatians 1:8-9

The language of Paul is very shocking. He is firm because He is defending an essential of Christian doctrine, which is the need to be saved alone by faith. But there will always be satanically sent men who will pervert the gospel and lead people astray.

He said to His disciples, "It is inevitable that stumbling blocks come, but woe to him through whom they come! It would be better for him if a millstone were hung around his neck and he were thrown into the sea, than that he would cause one of these little ones to stumble.

- Luke 17:1-2

It may be entirely possible that the reason you feel far from God is that you have been taught something contrary to what the Bible teaches, and so consequently have actually been serving a false god. You must look hard and honestly for the real truth until you find it.

If you have open ears and an honest heart, then you will find the truth. Jesus said that He is '*the Way,* **the Truth** *and the Life (John 14:6),*' if you want to know the truth, then you need to approach the God of Truth. That is if you really are interested in knowing the truth and obeying this same truth. If, however, you are intent on remaining in your sins, then you will invent your own facts to accommodate your lifestyle. This will only end very terribly for you if you persist in it.

One will ask, '*If we all believe in a Jesus does it actually matter if we don't all have the same beliefs about Him or God?*'. Well, consider the story of Jesus, revealing God to the Samaritan woman. He said more or less that the Samaritans didn't know whom they were worshipping (*John 4:22*) but that the Jews did – doctrinally the Samaritans only believed in the first five books of the Bible and therefore were in a terrible error. However, what did Jesus say to her about worshipping God?

But an hour is coming, and now is, when the true worshipers will

> worship the Father in spirit and truth; for such people the Father seeks to be His worshipers. God is spirit, and those who worship Him must worship in spirit and truth."
>
> - John 4:23-24

In a true worshipper's heart, there must be a balance of both the Spirit – which is talking about the Holy Spirit and truth to know the One who is worshipped. We need to be absolutely sure of the truth. To neglect either will destroy us.

It is said by some: "Well, if everybody who says they accept Jesus Christ all gets along despite what we believe about Him, what is wrong with that? We ought not to be narrow and bigoted in our thinking." - but listen to what Paul said to the Corinthians.

> But I am afraid that, as the serpent deceived Eve by his craftiness, your minds will be led astray from the simplicity and purity of devotion to Christ. For if one comes and preaches another Jesus whom we have not preached, or you receive a different spirit which you have not received, or a different gospel which you have not accepted, you bear this beautifully.
>
> - 2 Corinthians 11:3-4

Paul is saying here that the Church at Corinth was very accepting of these people with their apostate doctrine and was concerned that, because of this, they were going to be led astray.

This is why a careful approach is needed. There are today false teachers and those who do not preach or teach what is right. It is unfortunate that millions are deceived. But as it is today, so it was in the day of Jeremiah. Comfort is given to those who are in sin when it is a warning and not comfort that should be given.

> "They heal the brokenness of the daughter of My people superficially,
> **Saying, 'Peace, peace,'**
> **But there is no peace.**
> "Were they ashamed because of the abomination they had done? They certainly were not ashamed,

*And they did not know how to blush;
Therefore they shall fall among those who fall;
At the time of their punishment they shall be brought down,"
Says the Lord.*

- Jeremiah 8:11-12 (Emphasis added)

The Bible says very clearly that only those who conform to what God says will have His peace. Unity must be with those of the same Spirit, not just for the sake of peace. It is very dangerous to do otherwise.

"There is no peace for the wicked," says the Lord.

- Isaiah 48:22

To pray:

Father, I pray that You would, by the Holy Spirit, reveal the real Jesus to me. I acknowledge that I may be mistaken over who Jesus is. I want to know the real Jesus. Please give me the Holy Spirit to come and change me that I may become more like You. Help me also to read Your Bible daily so that I might learn what the truth is. In Jesus' Name, I pray. Amen.

CHAPTER THREE: SEEKING HIM

*When You said, "Seek My face,"
my heart said to You, "Your
face, O Lord, I shall seek."*

Psalm 27:8

It was always in the heart of God to be close to His people. In a real and tangible way as opposed to as some think, in some mystical and spiritual way. Far out of reach by many.

Draw near to God and He will draw near to you.

- James 4:8

How close someone is to God is dependent on the person concerned, not God. The Christian should make his relationship with God the most important part of his life. The greatest commandment is to love God completely. To set knowing Him as the main priority of life.

Unfortunately, within Christian circles, there has developed grave selfishness among Christians who have the attitude that God serves them as some kind of divine butler or a genie in a lamp to grant wishes, to bless and make one happy.

> *"No one can serve two masters; for either he will hate the one and love the other, or he will be devoted to one and despise the other. You cannot serve God and wealth.*
> - *Matthew 6:24*

No one can serve God and gain at the same time. Neither is it possible to serve God to increase. The motivation of the heart in these matters is very wrong, and Paul even writes about it to Timothy.

> *If anyone advocates a different doctrine and does not agree with sound words, those of our Lord Jesus Christ, and with the doctrine conforming to godliness, he is conceited and understands nothing; but he has a morbid interest in controversial questions and disputes about words, out of which arise envy, strife, abusive language, evil suspicions, and constant friction between men of depraved mind and deprived of the truth, **who suppose that godliness is a means of gain.** But godliness actually is a means of great gain when accompanied by contentment.*
> - *1 Timothy 6:3-6 (Emphasis added)*

In light of this passage, what then is God looking for in a man? What heart motivation is it that pleases Him?

> *He has told you, O man, what is good;*
> *And what does the Lord require of you*
> *But to do justice, to love kindness,*
> *And to walk humbly with your God?*
> - *Micah 6:8*

Act fairly, to be forgiving, kind and to be humble in walking with God. What does it mean by the term 'walk humbly?' Being humble is seen by many today as a weakness. But a Christian is to be meek, not weak. Being humble in a sense the Bible means it, is to have very high regard for God and not to think more highly of oneself than one ought to. It also means to consider more the concerns of others rather than one's own interests. In essence, to be meek is to love. It's imperative.

God is opposed to the proud, but gives grace to the humble."

- James 4:6

God will bypass proud and self-sufficient sinners and will not acknowledge them. The Pharisees, the scribes and the lawyers, for example, were people who were proud of their religious life. Meanwhile, those who are humble in heart and know that they need mercy, to them He grants forgiveness. These people are like the prostitutes, the tax collectors, and the sinners who feel the shame of their sin and are crying inside.

There is the matter of humbling oneself before God and seeking Him. Having His sweet fellowship is better than life itself.

You will make known to me the path of life;
In Your presence is fullness of joy;
In Your right hand there are pleasures forever.

- Psalm 16:11

It takes a great deal as with any relationship. The relationship you have with God must be cultivated by regular intimacy with Him. Cultivate according to the dictionary, as in to promote or improve the growth of (a plant, crop or in this case a relationship) by labour and attention.[2] Ask any gardener! Growing any kind of vegetation is not easy. You don't just scatter some seeds and leave it. No! It requires constant care and attention, either by watering or through protecting it from hungry, ravenous insects. Similarly, the soul must be spiritually watered by daily prayer and reading of the Bible. Also, guarding the heart against the devil's temptations and human nature is very much needed. God must come first. Do you spend hours with the internet and only minutes with God? As they say:

"Much prayer, much power. Little prayer, little power. No prayer, no power."

Now, could that be the reason for the seeming lack of power in the Western Church? It very well could be. Sometimes a close relationship with God requires that one will have to give up something or someone to be able to have it. If you are going to go on with God, then there are most certainly things in your life that you are going to have to lay down. There is no getting around this.

> *Then Jesus said to His disciples, "If anyone wishes to come after Me, he must deny himself, and take up his cross and follow Me. For whoever wishes to save his life will lose it; but whoever loses his life for My sake will find it. For what will it profit a man if he gains the whole world and forfeits his soul? Or what will a man give in exchange for his soul?*
>
> *- Matthew 16:24-26*

A massive idol for me personally speaking was the idol of having a dependency on other people. Instead of going straight to God, I would try to either spend time with people (usually girls), or I would speak with many people over the internet. The Lord brought upon me very sour relationships and allowed big problems between me and others until I learnt to lean only on Him. I learnt to hate my idolatry, and I had to cast it far away from me. I came off social media and based my worth on my relationship with God, not on what girls thought about me. However, it must be said that God had to bring about in my own heart a hatred of my idol until I couldn't stand it anymore.

He will do the same to you. Your relationship with Him is so precious to Him that He will not allow anything to get in the way of that relationship.

> *—for you shall not worship any other god, for the Lord, whose name is Jealous, is a jealous God—*
>
> *- Exodus 34:14*

God is to be number one of your life. For Him to be second to something else is unthinkable. No, God should always be first. Always. Anything less is disobedience.

In the Bible, there are some passages about the first king of Israel king Saul. Saul was a man who did not love God. He wanted to look good because his faith was shallow (*1 Samuel 15:30*); God was not first in his life. He had a form of godliness and looking good by appearance, but sadly lacked power.

A. W. Tozer wrote:

> *"Gifts and power for service the Spirit surely desires to impart; but holiness and spiritual worship come first."*[3]

If you want the power of God, you must go to the place that leads to it. Quality time alone with God and reading the Bible are the main two. God takes this kind of commitment very seriously.

For the kingdom of God does not consist in words but in power.
- 1 Corinthians 4:20

Having the appearance of power by words can be deceiving. Everything that is based only on appearance and not on a relationship with Christ is going to crumble in these coming days. Only the one with his foundations firm and his roots deep in the water of life will endure the future storms.

Consider the life and heart attitude of David. He had an inner longing for God that totally dominated his entire life. He was not satisfied with the status quo. He wasn't a man that had any love in his heart for anything more than God. Just look at some of these beautiful words he penned:

"I love You, O Lord, my strength."
The Lord is my rock and my fortress and my deliverer,
My God, my rock, in whom I take refuge;
My shield and the horn of my salvation, my stronghold.
- Psalm 18:1-2

O God, You are my God; I shall seek You earnestly;
My soul thirsts for You, my flesh yearns for You,
In a dry and weary land where there is no water.
- Psalm 63:1

I remember the days of old;
I meditate on all Your doings;
I muse on the work of Your hands.
I stretch out my hands to You;
My soul longs for You, as a parched land.
- Psalm 143:5-6

Now there was a man with an intense longing for God! He was tired of dry, empty religion. Jesus Himself said that *He who believes in Me, as the Scripture said, 'From his innermost being will flow rivers of living water (John 7:38).'* It must be noted here that Jesus is not talking about the intellectual head belief of acknowledgement of the facts. Instead, He is talking about heart belief, where the will of a person results in an action.

But someone may well say, "You have faith and I have works; show me your faith without the works, and I will show you my faith by my works."
- James 2:18

The rivers of living water that Jesus here refers to does not flow from those who have no sincere desire for Him. Remember what the Bible says of David – that he was a man after God's own heart (*1 Samuel 13:14*). What resulted from that for David?

Not only was he made king instead of Saul, but he was the greatest king that ever reigned over Israel and out of his descendants came the Messiah Jesus Christ. The Bible actually records in 1 Samuel 18 that Saul was afraid of David.

Saul despised God, and so God left Him and came to David. David had this blessing because God was number One in his heart. It sounds like such a cliché, but it's the truth of the matter.

> *But seek first His kingdom and His righteousness, and all these things will be added to you.*
>
> *- Matthew 6:33*

Here again, is the divine principle put forth by our Lord. God will take care of everything. He will move heaven and earth to meet the needs of a man that trusts Him and puts Him first.

There are very grave warnings given in the scriptures which we would be wise to heed. Given them, everyone who professes to know Him must spend time with Him. The danger to neglect this is far too great.

> *For if the word spoken through angels proved unalterable, and every transgression and disobedience received a just penalty,* **how will we escape if we neglect so great a salvation?**
>
> *- Hebrews 2:2-3 (Emphasis added)*

> *Many will say to Me on that day, 'Lord, Lord, did we not prophesy in Your name, and in Your name cast out demons, and in Your name perform many miracles?' And then I will declare to them, 'I never knew you; depart from Me, you who practice lawlessness.'*
>
> *- Matthew 7:22-23*

To pray:

"Father, I confess that I have not been seeking You as I should. I make a commitment that I will try to put You first every day before everything else. I will try to set time aside for quality time with You. Only help me to not slip into apathy and to do this. I love You and want nothing to get in the way of our relationship. In Jesus' Name. Amen"

CHAPTER FOUR: TO OBEY

The Lord is my portion; I have promised to keep Your words.

Psalm 119:57

Obeying God is not a choice that is given to His people. Jesus said that if a person was to really love Him then he would obey His commandments (John 14:15).

"Come now, and let us reason together,"
Says the Lord,
"Though your sins are as scarlet,
They will be as white as snow;
Though they are red like crimson,
They will be like wool.
"If you consent and obey,
You will eat the best of the land;
"But if you refuse and rebel,
You will be devoured by the sword."
Truly, the mouth of the Lord has spoken.
- Isaiah 1:18-20

Here is the invitation for forgiveness, but with it, comes a warning, because there does come a time when God says 'Enough!'. He is willing, so willing, to forgive - but if His generous offer of a free pardon is repeatedly rejected, then a day will eventually come when God will lift His hand of mercy and bring down His hand of judgement.

And this is precisely what happened. God rose up the Babylonians who came and literally levelled Jerusalem and took the people away captive. They lived in captivity for the next seventy years, most of them dying in that captivity. It was the result of being disobedient to God and refusing to amend their ways and turning from sin. Despite what the enemy says, there is always a consequence for disobeying God.

> *By the rivers of Babylon,*
> *There we sat down and wept,*
> *When we remembered Zion.*
>
> *- Psalm 137:1*

There are Christians who say that, because we are under the New Covenant, we don't have to worry about all those rules, for God is merciful. However, you will not find this attitude at all in the minds of the New Testament writers. This is grace presumed.

> *But it is easier for heaven and earth to pass away than for one stroke of a letter of the Law to fail.*
>
> *- Luke 16:17*

The above statement is not what it may appear to be. On the surface, it may seem that Jesus is implying something legalistic. Yet this was not the case. You see, the law that Jesus came to get rid of was the ceremonial law (*see Hebrews 10:1-18*). Because He died for our sins, rose again from the dead after three days and now sits at the right hand of God as the Christian's eternal High Priest, one doesn't have to go through the law's prescribed method of approaching God. That is, to make sacrifices and go through the High Priest on the Day of Atonement (The only day a year when the High Priest would go into the Temple right into the Holy of holies where God was, to intercede for himself and the people).

The law that God still requires Christians today to keep is God's moral law. Which is essentially what God commands in the realm of morality, what is right, acceptable, and what is wrong and not. An example is the Ten Commandments. Those are the basis for the moral law - which can be summed up in loving God and loving our neighbour as ourselves. He also expects us to keep the royal law.

> *If, however, you are fulfilling the royal law according to the Scripture, "You shall love your neighbor as yourself," you are doing well.*
>
> *- James 2:8*

Legalism in its most accurate definition is a man-made religious system of using works to build righteousness before God that does not come by faith - but true righteousness and the only righteousness that God acknowledges comes only by faith. That is that it is received as a free gift, and the Spirit of God comes to live in a person and transforms them to help them practically in their day to day lives to be righteous. This is the process of being saved.

> *So then, my beloved, just as you have always obeyed, not as in my presence only, but now much more in my absence, work out your salvation with fear and trembling.*
>
> *- Philippians 2:12*

This is the on-going work of the Holy Spirit when He is given to them at the moment of conversion to make them more like Jesus Christ – holy. He does this by writing the law on the heart and in the mind so that it is reasonable to act righteously (*Jeremiah 31:33-34*).

That's why when people come to Him, they change -because the Spirit of God is writing the law on their hearts, they slowly begin to change on the inside. Considering this, one can see from the lifestyle of a person if indeed this has taken place. It is impossible to have changed life and not have a changed lifestyle.

Before a Christian is regenerated (that is before coming to Christ, regeneration is what happens the moment the life is given to Christ – He regenerates the person and makes their spirit alive – being born again) it could not be helped – sin was always inevitable. It is part of who the person is, but when the Holy Spirit comes, they are no longer a slave to sin but a slave to God. And that sin is no longer part of who the person is.

It's not that they become entirely sinless – instead, the relationship with sin has changed. There is no more extended peace with sin. Rather now, instead it is hated, and war is waged against it by the individual. There are new desires to please God and obey Him. Grace, therefore, is not a licence to sin.

> *but like the Holy One who called you, be holy yourselves also in all your behavior; because it is written, "You shall be holy, for I am holy."*
>
> *- 1 Peter 1:15-16*

This shows God's heart on the matter. Holiness must be the pursuit of everyone who claims to be Christian.

> *Do not be deceived, God is not mocked; for whatever a man sows, this he will also reap. For the one who sows to his own flesh will from the flesh reap corruption, but the one who sows to the Spirit will from the Spirit reap eternal life.*
>
> *- Galatians 6:7-8*

There are consequences for how life is lived. It is sombre. Nobody can live as they please and then expect to go to heaven when they die. The warnings of the Bible make it very clear, despite what anyone might say.

Let no one deceive you with empty words, for because of these things the wrath of God comes upon the sons of disobedience. Therefore do not be partakers with them.
- Ephesians 5:6-7

You were running well; who hindered you from obeying the truth? This persuasion did not come from Him who calls you.
- Galatians 5:7-8

Sometimes people even assume that if good work is done for God, then it will appease Him. That somehow, God will overlook their transgression of His commandments because of their piety. Yet they don't think this same way about civil law. If that kind of thinking will not stick in a court of law today, then why do some presume it will work for God? Maybe because He is a God of love some think He will turn a blind eye – but this is a misunderstanding of who God is.

Samuel said,

"Has the Lord as much delight in burnt offerings and sacrifices
As in obeying the voice of the Lord?
Behold, to obey is better than sacrifice,
And to heed than the fat of rams.
"For rebellion is as the sin of divination,
And insubordination is as iniquity and idolatry.
Because you have rejected the word of the Lord,
He has also rejected you from being king."
- 1 Samuel 15:22-23

No, rebellion whatever excuse or reason that is given is totally and utterly unacceptable to God. Obeying what God says is more important to Him than any 'good' thing we may do for Him.

Then some Pharisees and scribes came to Jesus from Jerusalem

> *and said, "Why do Your disciples break the tradition of the elders? For they do not wash their hands when they eat bread." And He answered and said to them, "Why do you yourselves transgress the commandment of God for the sake of your tradition? For God said, 'Honor your father and mother,' and, 'He who speaks evil of father or mother is to be put to death.' But you say, 'Whoever says to his father or mother, "Whatever I have that would help you has been given to God," he is not to honor his father or his mother.' And by this you invalidated the word of God for the sake of your tradition.*
>
> *- Matthew 15:1-6*

The Pharisees and the teachers of the law were only interested in an outward appearance of righteousness. They had nothing of the power of God that brings that inner change. They said that it was okay to dishonour one's parents if one was using what would have gone to their parents to give to God - but you can't fool God.

Suppose you are going to church and someone is in desperate need. Do you think it would please God if you turned that person away because you are busy 'serving' God? The answer should be undeniable.

> *But whoever has the world's goods, and sees his brother in need and closes his heart against him, how does the love of God abide in him?*
>
> *- 1 John 3:17*

It is often forgotten that a holy life is expected by God. Jesus Christ and His example must be imitated (*1 John 4:17*). So how did Jesus Christ live His life?

> *"I can do nothing on My own initiative. As I hear, I judge; and My judgment is just, because I do not seek My own will, but the will of Him who sent Me.*
>
> *- John 5:30*

He always lived in complete submission to the Father. He did not go around doing His own will. Likewise, the Christian is also to live in submission to God.

In fact, I had a friend, a Christian friend, who had argued with me about sex before marriage. He maintained that it was acceptable to sleep with someone before marriage. He gave me a great list of reasons why it was okay and how the Bible didn't really mean what it says. Essentially, taking the Bible and distorting it to make something right that the Bible calls wrong (*2 Peter 3:15-16*).

This is a hazardous practice, for sin has its consequences. These are people that have practices in their lives that the Bible speaks against, but instead of repenting of and forsaking these practices, they take the Bible and twist its meaning so that they don't have to obey what it is really saying. They do this because they have embraced sin and made peace with it. Yet the Bible is clear on the matter and indeed speaks for itself. You have to read and obey what you read, it will eternally ruin you if you try to twist it.

Sometimes, to be obedient to God, it will cause one to go against what the government says. This is not advocating rebellion towards ruling authorities as to the Bible actually teaches submission towards the government (*Romans 13:1-7* & *1 Peter 2:13-17*). However, when there is a contradiction between two commandments, one that God tells you that you should do and one the government tells you that you should do, then it is better for you to obey God rather than people. It will cost you for standing up for Christ and following Him, but there is a sure reward for those who acknowledge Him before men (*Matthew 10:32-33*).

> *When they had brought them, they stood them before the Council. The high priest questioned them, saying, "We gave you strict orders not to continue teaching in this name, and yet, you have filled Jerusalem with your teaching and intend to bring this man's*

blood upon us." But Peter and the apostles answered, "We must obey God rather than men.

- Acts 5:27-29

If God is speaking to you about any questionable practices in your life, obey Him and put them away. Don't try to make it right when it is wrong. Don't try and offer up something to God instead of doing what He says. Don't ignore Him. There is only so much mercy God will give before He acts in judgement. Please do it today.

But encourage one another day after day, as long as it is still called "Today," so that none of you will be hardened by the deceitfulness of sin. For we have become partakers of Christ, if we hold fast the beginning of our assurance firm until the end, while it is said,

"Today if you hear His voice,
Do not harden your hearts, as when they provoked Me."

- Hebrews 3:13-15

To pray:

"Father, I come to You to ask your forgiveness for the times when I have not obeyed You. Help me to listen to what You say and then to put it into practice. I want to be an obedient child. I don't want to make any more excuses. Help me to live a life that is pleasing to You. I ask it in Jesus' Name. Amen."

CHAPTER FIVE: RECONCILIATION WITH OTHERS

And the seed whose fruit is righteousness is sown in peace by those who make peace

James 3:18

The one word that sums up God's plan for mankind is reconciliation. In the dictionary, reconciliation is defined as an act of reconciling, as when former enemies agree to an amicable (goodwill, friendly, peaceable) truce.4

Paul said to the Corinthians *'be reconciled to God,'"* (*2 Corinthians 5:20*). The whole purpose of the coming of the Lord Jesus Christ was to reconcile us to God.

> *And although you were formerly alienated and hostile in mind, engaged in evil deeds, yet He has now reconciled you in His fleshly body through death, in order to present you before Him holy and blameless and beyond reproach—*
>
> *- Colossians 1:21-22*

There is another kind of reconciliation that is important to know about. Just as the Bible makes it very clear that to be forgiven by God, forgiving others is a must, also after being reconciled to God Christians need to be reconciled to one another. Consider the following:

Therefore if you are presenting your offering at the altar, and there remember that your brother has something against you, leave your offering there before the altar and go; first be reconciled to your brother, and then come and present your offering.

- Matthew 5:23-24

In other words, Christ is saying here that before approaching God with worship making peace with others must come first. God's peace does not come to those who have enmity and war with others.

What is the source of quarrels and conflicts among you? Is not the source your pleasures that wage war in your members? You lust and do not have; so you commit murder. You are envious and cannot obtain; so you fight and quarrel. You do not have because you do not ask. You ask and do not receive, because you ask with wrong motives, so that you may spend it on your pleasures.

- James 4:1-3

Remember that in the Bible, King David was a very righteous man. Now he had a desire to build God a temple – a great passion. Despite this, God would not permit him. Not because there was any sin in his heart at that time or any need to be reconciled to anyone. God called David a man of war; therefore, he was not allowed to build the temple because he had spilt much blood (*See 2 Samuel 7 for the full story*). He was excluded from his desire because he was a man of war.

"*Blessed are the peacemakers, for they shall be called sons of God.*

- Matthew 5:9

In my personal life, when I first became a Christian, I was very involved with the Church, but I had a problem – I despised and hated my brother. As I was looking for a 'word' from God during this time, I received one! It was '**Repent!**' The Lord cut me down so much for this sin. I knew He was angry with me for my attitude.

You see, a religion that is not accompanied by love for one's brother is worthless. God cares how His people treat others, He is not concerned with outward appearances as much as He is with the heart and its intentions.

"You sit and speak against your brother;
You slander your own mother's son.
"These things you have done and I kept silence;
You thought that I was just like you;
I will reprove you and state the case in order before your eyes.
- Psalm 50:20-21

My brother and I have a much closer relationship than we ever had before. The reason is simply that God asks us as Christians not just to be reconciled to Him, but to each other as well.

Behold, how good and how pleasant it is
For brothers to dwell together in unity!
It is like the precious oil upon the head,
Coming down upon the beard,
Even Aaron's beard,
Coming down upon the edge of his robes.
It is like the dew of Hermon
Coming down upon the mountains of Zion;
For there the Lord commanded the blessing—life forever.
- Psalm 133:1-3 (Emphasis added)

Notice that the Lord commanded the blessing when brethren dwell together in unity – *'for there the Lord commanded the blessing.'* When God's people live together in harmony with one another and put things right with one another – that is where God's blessing is. Yet it is not the unity of all religions that is the focus here. That is impossible (when this does appear to happen, know for sure that it is antichrist). No, unity has to be grounded in truth. That is unity in Christ and His Bible. Not unity for the sake of unity.

> *being diligent to preserve the unity of the Spirit in the bond of peace.*
>
> *- Ephesians 4:3*

In the Bible, Paul writes a letter to Philemon – a slave owner concerning a runaway slave called Onesimus. This particular slave had been converted by Paul (*Philemon 10*) no doubt in Rome as the city was full of runaway slaves. Paul had written to Philemon sending Onesimus back to him. This passage has been misused and abused to show that the Bible is in favour of slavery. But the main focus is actually one of reconciliation between Philemon and Onesimus. Paul sent Onesimus back to Philemon to that he could put things right between himself and Philemon. Furthermore, Paul urged Philemon to not only forgive Onesimus, but to take him back – not as a slave, but as a fellow brother! They were Christians, both!

> *For perhaps he was for this reason separated from you for a while, that you would have him back forever, no longer as a slave, but more than a slave, a beloved brother, especially to me, but how much more to you, both in the flesh and in the Lord. If then you regard me a partner, accept him as you would me.*
>
> *- Philemon 1:15-17*

Whatever the relationship between Philemon and Onesimus had existed before this – Paul was seeking both of them to be reconciled. Reconciliation, not slavery was the issue at hand here.

If you have an on-going feud with someone – big or small, put it right with them.

Pursue peace with all men.

- Hebrews 12:14

Be angry, and yet do not sin; do not let the sun go down on your anger.

- Ephesians 4:26

Never, ever put off making up with someone until the next day. What happens if either of you dies in your sleep? How will you put things right then? Make every effort to be reconciled today because tomorrow is not promised to you! It may be that the reason God feels distant from you is that you are holding onto a grudge against someone, or that there are ill feelings between you and someone else. It may not be possible to live at peace with them, but on your part, you should make every effort. How can you claim to serve the God of reconciliation if you are unwilling to be reconciled with others?

I had a Youth Pastor over me once while I was a young teenager in the Church. I was very arrogant in my ways and incredibly worldly. I didn't have any respect for authority (This will be covered in Chapter Seven), and I disrespected her as a Youth Pastor. God began dealing with me about this issue, and I made peace with her and reconciled myself to her by going to her and apologising. You see, sometimes to do the right thing, you will have to get over yourself and apologise to people. Even if they ought to say sorry to you-you cannot take for granted that they will say sorry back. It's not your concern if they don't; your matter is to do what God wants you to do. Forgive them and leave them to God. If you try to be reconciled and the other person isn't interested in being reconciled to you, then it's their problem. You have done what is right and pleasing before God.

Above all, keep fervent in your love for one another, because love covers a multitude of sins.

- 1 Peter 4:8

To pray:

"Father, please forgive me for having a problem between this person and me. After I have received Your forgiveness for this sin, help me to go to the person and put it right. I know this is pleasing in Your sight. I thank You that you have reconciled me to Yourself now help me to be reconciled to others that I may be a good representation of the heart of God in reaching out to others in love. In Jesus' Name. Amen.

CHAPTER SIX: UNFORGIVENESS

bearing with one another, and forgiving each other, whoever has a complaint against anyone; just as the Lord forgave you, so also should you.

Colossians 3:13

All of the scripture attests to the loving-kindness of God. He is a God Who forgives.

If You, Lord, should mark iniquities,
O Lord, who could stand?
But there is forgiveness with You,
That You may be feared.
          - Psalm 130:3-4

Forgiveness of sins is the central theme here because there is the ultimate question a person must answer: Whether they have been forgiven by God. This is more important and carries with it far more weight than any other matter in life.

Obviously, it should be clear by now that the only way to be forgiven is through Jesus Christ and His cross. It is crucial to know that God does give us assurance of being forgiven.

> *If anyone sees his brother committing a sin not leading to death, he shall ask and God will for him give life to those who commit sin not leading to death. There is a sin leading to death; I do not say that he should make request for this. All unrighteousness is sin, and there is a sin not leading to death.*
>
> *- 1 John 5:16-17*

Of course, there is no need to go into the deep theological meanings behind that passage and have opened up to you the different types of sin there are. But what needs to be kept in mind is that certain sins do lead to death, i.e., spiritual death, eternal hell.

Unforgiveness is a spiritual killer. It is undeniable if you read the Bible, but alas, there is a real difference between knowing what is written and actually living by what is written.

Many years ago, when I was just a small boy, my mother was a member of a particular Church. A message was given by a preacher on the topic of Unforgiveness. Afterwards, an appeal was made for people to come forward who have harboured Unforgiveness and who needed to repent of it. Shockingly, considering that learning to forgive others as it seems, is one of the very basics of the Christian faith, about half the church went up for prayer! Later I learnt that there were also feuds and unresolved conflicts going on. Christian was refusing to sit next to Christian because of such and such reasons. This type of behaviour brings reproach upon the whole body of Christ.

> *By this all men will know that you are My disciples, if you have love for one another."*
>
> *- John 13:35*

God commands us to forgive each other and be reconciled to one another. Jesus' teaching is unambiguous on the matter, so how could they have completely missed it?

There are two main reasons for this:

1. Despite claiming to be Bible-believing Christians, they don't read their Bibles.

There are all sorts of reasons people don't read their Bibles. Neglecting the Bible is dangerous because you will not be able to know what is right and what is not false. To be honest, almost every reason for not reading the Bible is an excuse. You must make time. For this reason, unforgiveness is missed.

2. Despite reading the Bible when they come to passages on unforgiveness, they persuade themselves that they are justified to hold onto their grudge.

"They hurt me so much that I cannot lay down the hurt," and so because they have been hurt quite severely, they feel it is okay for them to hold on to the anger.

Scripture tells us we ought to walk after the same manner that Jesus walked on the earth, to live as Jesus lived (*1 John 2:6*). When Jesus was crucified and put to death by the hands of those He created what was His response? Did He cry out in anger and vow vengeance from on high? No.

But Jesus was saying, "Father, forgive them; for they do not know what they are doing."

- Luke 23:34

He is the example of how the Christian is to live. The very word Christian means 'little-Christ.' The implication is for the Christian to be Christ-like.

For if you forgive others for their transgressions, your heavenly Father will also forgive you. But if you do not forgive others, then your Father will not forgive your transgressions.

- Mathew 6:14-15

Bear in mind that this isn't just any teacher; this is the Prince of Life Himself. No lie will ever be found on His lips (*Hebrews 6:18*).

Ask yourself if you have unforgiveness in your heart. You will find that unforgiveness will be a barrier between you and God. God won't hear your prayers if you refuse to forgive others. People sigh and cry that God feels distant from them, yet they hold onto their grudges. They refuse to put things right with others. To put into context for you, that is to show you the deepness of this sin – consider the following:

> *"You have heard that the ancients were told, 'You shall not commit murder' and 'Whoever commits murder shall be liable to the court.' But I say to you that everyone who is angry with his brother shall be guilty before the court; and whoever says to his brother, 'You good-for-nothing,' shall be guilty before the supreme court; and whoever says, 'You fool,' shall be guilty enough to go into the fiery hell.*
>
> – Matthew 5:21-22

In God's eyes, hatred is the same evil as murder just as lust is on a par with adultery because these issues spring from the heart.

> *Everyone who hates his brother is a murderer; and you know that no murderer has eternal life abiding in him.*
>
> – 1 John 3:15

All the evil that people do comes ultimately from their hearts. That's the issue here. Unforgiveness is essentially saying – 'that person doesn't deserve my forgiveness,' God Who knows the thoughts and intents of the heart (*Psalm 44:21*) will respond in the same way towards you. And you don't want that to happen!

It is imperative to always be ready to forgive those who sin against you as taught in the parable of the unforgiving servant. See Matthew 18 and Matthew 6:14-15, which demonstrates that the forgiveness a Christian extends **must** mirror that of the

Father's.

Even if the offender himself doesn't repent or show any remorse for his actions against you, you should still have peace knowing that vengeance belongs to God alone. Paul gives an example:

Alexander the coppersmith did me much harm; the Lord will repay him according to his deeds. Be on guard against him yourself, for he vigorously opposed our teaching.

- 2 Timothy 4:14-15

Christians should love their enemies and do them good, which is commended by scripture:

*Repay no one evil for evil. Have regard for good things in the sight of all men. If it is possible, as much as depends on you, live peaceably with all men. Beloved, do not avenge yourselves, but rather give place to wrath; for it is written, "**Vengeance is Mine, I will repay**," says the Lord. **Therefore "If your enemy is hungry, feed him; if he is thirsty, give him a drink; for in so doing you will heap coals of fire on his head**." Do not be overcome by evil, but overcome evil with good.*

- Romans 12:17-21 (Emphasis added)

Some preachers say that having unforgiveness towards someone does not affect salvation – in other words, that it does not mean we won't be forgiven it just means we won't be free from the bondage of it. But this is not at all what the Bible says. You cannot support such a view in light of the teaching of the Bible because it contradicts what the Bible plainly says, which is very clear. **If you don't forgive other people, you will not be forgiven by God.** It really is that simple.

Many people teach contrary to this. They try to make the Word of God appear softer than it actually is. They don't like the thought of repentance to receive forgiveness and assure us that God's mercy is free regardless of how one comes to God. They also don't like the idea of a God who avenges. So they, therefore, fail to teach by what the Bible says:

A jealous and avenging God is the Lord;
The Lord is avenging and wrathful.
The Lord takes vengeance on His adversaries,
And He reserves wrath for His enemies.

- Nahum 1:2

Namely, they teach that God's forgiveness comes regardless of repentance or whether or not one forgives others. Purportedly people need counselling for being grieved by others but what they really need is to forgive the offender and let go of the grudge they hold. This, of course, does not account for all of the problems concerned as there is a great deal many others.

We must forgive one another. I have learnt how to forgive because God brought some people into my life who hurt me, and were never sorry for having hurt me. These people are Christians and really love the Lord, so in my mind, I am thinking, *'how can they hurt me and not even feel sorry for this? These people are Christians!'*

However, God told me that when He looks at me, He doesn't see me through my sin. Instead, when He looks at me, he sees no sin because as far as He is concerned, I have not sinned – I am in Christ. In the same way, I have to look at these Christian brothers and sisters in the same way. Also, there was an occasion when I was praying to God about a particular person, and I said more or less that I forgave them, but I didn't want to talk to them because I didn't trust them. The Holy Spirit replied to me in the following way:

> "*I want you to build a bridge between you and this person. Make friends with them. As I built a bridge between you and me so that we could become friends.*"

It was, by no means, easy. Everything in me raged against what God told me to do. Make friends with someone who destroyed me? Build a bridge with someone who made me the centre of gossip among all the women? It may be a small matter to you but at the time that all of this happened - it broke me into a million pieces. Since those days until now, I have never been so low in my personal, emotional and spiritual life as I was at that moment.

I admit that it was almost impossible for me to do what God asked, but He helped me. And with his strength, I was able to love someone who did not love me back. It is not easy, but when you think about how much God has forgiven you, it becomes easier to forgive others. To love in the same way that Christ loves you, which can only be done with the help of the Holy Spirit. Forgiving others frees you from your own prison of bitterness. Holding onto unforgiveness is a burden. You must leave your hurts at the foot of the cross and allow Him to heal your broken heart.

To pray:

"Father, thank You so much for the forgiveness that is available to me because of the cross. In the same way that You have forgiven me and have taken my sin and dropped it into Your ocean of forgetfulness forever help me to do exactly that with everyone who has sinned against me. May there be no traces of unforgiveness in me towards any of my relatives, friends or enemies. I forgive the wrongs that all these people may have done against me. I will remember it no more. In Jesus' Name. Amen."

CHAPTER SEVEN: REBELLION

A rebellious man seeks only evil, so a cruel messenger will be sent against him.

Proverbs 17:11

Rebellion is an attitude of people who more or less believe that "no one has a right to tell me what to do". Yet this is not the attitude that should be part of the Christian's character.

> **"For rebellion is as the sin of divination,**
> **And insubordination is as iniquity and idolatry.**
> Because you have rejected the word of the Lord,
> He has also rejected you from being king."
> - 1 Samuel 15:23 (Emphasis added)

You see here how God is comparing rebellion to occultic practices, something very shocking, to say the least. But the two are very closely related. To give you a fuller understanding of the way God views rebellion, it will be best to look at a story in the Old Testament. After God led the Israelites out of the desert by the hand of Moses, there was a man by the name of Korah who along with a few others, rose up against Moses leadership. God arranged for him and his 250 men to meet with Him along with Moses and Aaron in the sight of all Israel. This was for God to declare His thoughts on them rebelling against Moses and usurping his authority. What happened to these men? Did God take their rebellion lightly?

> *So they and all that belonged to them went down alive to Sheol; and the earth closed over them, and they perished from the midst of the assembly.*
>
> *- Numbers 16:33*

When you rebel against a man God appoints as a leader, you are rebelling against Him. This is incredibly serious! God regards the way His leaders are treated very seriously.

> *"Do not touch My anointed ones,*
> *And do My prophets no harm."*
> *- Psalm 105:15*

From the New Testament, there is a different story which should also serve as a grave warning. Acts 5 is a story about Ananias and Sapphira. They both decide to sell a piece of property but to lay only some of the money at the Apostles feet and to pretend that it was the full amount. They were trying to look good in front of everyone and were actually lying to God. Peter rebuked him for it. So how did this all play out?

> *And as he heard these words, Ananias fell down and breathed his last; and great fear came over all who heard of it. The young men got up and covered him up, and after carrying him out, they buried him.*
>
> *Now there elapsed an interval of about three hours, and his wife came in, not knowing what had happened. And Peter responded to her, "Tell me whether you sold the land for such and such a*

> *price?" And she said, "Yes, that was the price." Then Peter said to her, "Why is it that you have agreed together to put the Spirit of the Lord to the test? Behold, the feet of those who have buried your husband are at the door, and they will carry you out as well." And immediately she fell at his feet and breathed her last, and the young men came in and found her dead, and they carried her out and buried her beside her husband. And great fear came over the whole church, and over all who heard of these things.*
>
> *- Acts 5:5-11*

That was New Testament Christianity, and they died by the hand of God. They rebelled against God by lying to His face. The Bible paints a very full picture of God. It is not comfortable for the average person to think about, but the reality is made very clear. He is a compassionate God full of love, mercy and grace. But He is also a holy God, and it must be remembered that He is both love and holiness at the same time. God hates rebellion, and this is why He was extreme in His judgements.

> *You younger men, likewise, be subject to your elders; and all of you, clothe yourselves with humility toward one another, for God is opposed to the proud, but gives grace to the humble.*
>
> *- 1 Peter 5:5*

The Bible calls Christians to submit to one another. If they fight and argue over positions, then they are no different from how the world operates. The Church is supposed to be the light of the world (*Matthew 5:14*), so she ought to live differently to how the world lives.

One of the problem's with today's culture is this rebellion against one's parents. Everywhere it is pushed forward, even on Television young people are smarter than their parents and to the degree that it is actually cool to disobey and disrespect them. Young person, please listen to me. If you want to please your Father in heaven, you must not disrespect your parents. Don't follow the example of your peers or the culture around you but listen to what the Bible says. For it is a good long life for you if you will obey it's teaching.

> *Children, obey your parents in the Lord, for this is right. Honor your father and mother (which is the first commandment with a promise), so that it may be well with you, and that you may live long on the earth.*
>
> *- Ephesians 6:1-3*

The Bible promises long life to children who honour their parents. The truth is that God sees everything you do. He sees you when you do good but He also equally sees if you do not honour your parents. Please bear in mind that God always sees what you do.

The Bible also doesn't support a rebellion in any other kind of position either. As a citizen of a country or as a slave:

> *Slaves, be obedient to those who are your masters according to the flesh, with fear and trembling, in the sincerity of your heart, as to Christ; not by way of eyeservice, as men-pleasers, but as slaves of Christ, doing the will of God from the heart. With good will render service, as to the Lord, and not to men, knowing that whatever good thing each one does, this he will receive back from the Lord, whether slave or free.*
>
> *- Ephesians 6:5-8*

Of course, this is one of the many texts that people use to say that the Bible advocates slavery. People often seem to forget the issue at hand here. A Christian's job is to be a light and to share the love of Jesus wherever he goes (whether they are slave or free). If he rebels against his non-Christian master, then what would he think of Christianity? What would they think of God? For the sake of the salvation of masters, Christian slaves are to live humbly under them that they may lead them to Christ.

> *Every person is to be in subjection to the governing authorities. For there is no authority except from God, and those which exist*

are established by God. Therefore whoever resists authority has opposed the ordinance of God; and they who have opposed will receive condemnation upon themselves. For rulers are not a cause of fear for good behavior, but for evil. Do you want to have no fear of authority? Do what is good and you will have praise from the same; for it is a minister of God to you for good. But if you do what is evil, be afraid; for it does not bear the sword for nothing; for it is a minister of God, an avenger who brings wrath on the one who practices evil. Therefore it is necessary to be in subjection, not only because of wrath, but also for conscience' sake.

- Romans 13:1-5

Very clearly, a submission to the government and those in authority is required by God. The Bible teaches very clearly that governments are in place because God has put them there. This is to keep order and stability in society. Look at the following passage from Judges.

In those days there was no king in Israel; every man did what was right in his own eyes.

- Judges 17:6

Two chapters later in chapter 19 many men of the tribe of Benjamin surrounded a house that had recently lodged a stranger and they acted just like Sodom (*Genesis 19:5*) because they wanted to rape the man who was visiting. They ended up gang raping his female servant with such violence that she died as a result! When this had happened, and it had all come out into the open, the rest of the Benjamites refused to hand the men over. This led to a civil war which nearly wiped out the tribe of Benjamin!

Law and order are needed. But those in control at Paul's times were the Romans, and Paul was imprisoned and eventually killed (according to Church tradition) by the hands of the Romans. So isn't it weird that he said Christians ought to respect them? Not at all. Christians are to submit to the government – the only time when a Christian is not to submit to them is where the government is advocating something that is clearly against the Word of God. Remember, this planet and its kingdoms are only here for a brief moment. Those who are trying to overthrow the government are not only rebelling against God by attacking an institution He put in place but are also showing earthly-mindedness.

> *Jesus answered, "My kingdom is not of this world. If My kingdom were of this world, then My servants would be fighting so that I would not be handed over to the Jews; but as it is, My kingdom is not of this realm."*
>
> *- John 18:36*

The chief end of a Christian is to live for the kingdom of God. At this time it is a spiritual kingdom, and although His Kingdom is being lived out among His people there is yet to come in the future a fuller physical aspect of His reign being that He will be literally physically present ruling from Jerusalem. This day is coming soon. So, one must live in submission to all people that they might be brought into the Kingdom by a godly example. The Kingdom and Country that Christians belong to are most certainly not to be spread by political uprisings.

> *'Not by might nor by power, but by My Spirit,' says the Lord of hosts.*
>
> *- Zechariah 4:6*

Rebellion is what characterises the devil. It is hard because everything in human nature is naturally rebellious. But with God's help, one can indeed put away rebellion and live a life submitted to God and those in authority to live like the Son of God Jesus Christ.

> *Fools, because of their rebellious way,*
> *And because of their iniquities, were afflicted.*
>
> *- Psalm 107:17*

To pray:

"Father, forgive me for the rebellion in my heart. I recognise that this kind of behaviour is evil in Your sight. Help me to submit myself to those in authority over me. Whether it is the government over me, whether it is my boss at work or whether it is my Pastor or spiritual leader. I am sorry for the way I have been, help me to live a life of submission as Jesus lived. Help me to put to death this rebellious attitude of mine and to live for You alone. In Jesus' Name. Amen."

CHAPTER EIGHT: PRIDE, THE CHRISTIAN'S ENEMY

*For though the Lord is exalted,
yet He regards the lowly, but the
haughty He knows from afar.*

Psalm 138:6

The most serious sin anyone can ever harbour is the sin of pride. Remember that it was because of pride that Lucifer became satan.

*"Your heart was lifted up because of your beauty;
You corrupted your wisdom by reason of your splendor.
I cast you to the ground;
I put you before kings,
That they may see you.*

- Ezekiel 28:17

God threw satan out of Heaven, and one day, he will be consigned to hell forever. The Bible declares that the human heart is incredibly evil.

> *"The heart is more deceitful than all else*
> *And is desperately sick;*
> *Who can understand it?"*
>
> *- Jeremiah 17:9*

Humans are not, as they say, "basically good." No, everyone, since Adam and Eve, was born with this sinful nature which gives them an inner inclination to sin, that is to follow as it were the evil desires of their heart. There is a natural bent towards evil.

What happens when you ask any person whether they believe when they die, they will go to Heaven or hell? Regardless of any faith in Jesus Christ, most of them would assume that they are going to go to Heaven. How so?

The answer is pride. They each pride themselves on the fact that they're good people.

> *And someone came to Him and said, "Teacher, what good thing shall I do that I may obtain eternal life?" And He said to him, "Why are you asking Me about what is good? There is only One who is good; but if you wish to enter into life, keep the commandments."*
>
> *- Matthew 19:16-17*

God declares plainly that all people are sinners (*Romans 3:9*), but people believe that they can create their own righteousness instead of trusting in the finished work of the cross.

> *Behold, all you who kindle a fire,*
> *Who encircle yourselves with firebrands,*
> *Walk in the light of your fire*
> *And among the brands you have set ablaze.*
> *This you will have from My hand:*
> *You will lie down in torment.*

- Isaiah 50:11

So it is with all who hold onto their pride and refuse God's provision (Jesus Christ) and instead try to get to Heaven by their own efforts. They shall lie down in great torment which of course is to say in hell.

He who trusts in his own heart is a fool,
But he who walks wisely will be delivered.
- Proverbs 28:26

There is a trap laid out for Christians that many are not aware of. It is drilled into young people, for instance, that they are fantastic; that God is really pleased with them; that they can do anything, etc. It is an attempt by misled but sincere Christians to put self-confidence within Christian young people. The motivation is right, they do it to build up and edify young people to help them with their self-esteem and confidence. It is really understandable to be honest, as we all need building up. But the enemy subtly uses it to feed their emotions. There is, as a result, a whole generation of Christians who feel they can conquer the world for Jesus and yet it is all confidence in the flesh, that is to say, confidence in their own abilities and talents.

Thus says the Lord,
"Cursed is the man who trusts in mankind
And makes flesh his strength,
And whose heart turns away from the Lord.
- Jeremiah 17:5

*for we are the true circumcision, who worship in the Spirit of God and **glory in Christ Jesus and put no confidence in the flesh**.*
- Philippians 3:3 (Emphasis added)

That is where the mistake lies, in this '*I can do it! We're great! We're amazing, and we'll get through this!*' attitude. **No!** That is pride. Paul said there must be no confidence in that which is solely within a person. Where did Paul place his confidence? What did Paul glory in? In Christ Jesus.

For it is not you that's going to get you through but Christ in you!

> *I am the vine, you are the branches; he who abides in Me and I in him, he bears much fruit,* **for apart from Me you can do nothing.**
>
> - John 15:5 (Emphasis added)

> *But may it never be that I would boast, except in the cross of our Lord Jesus Christ, through which the world has been crucified to me, and I to the world.*
>
> - Galatians 6:14

The one thing that Paul boasted in was the cross of Jesus Christ. It may seem very cute and clichéd, but the cross that Paul was talking about was very barbaric. It is forgotten because today in the West, there is no crucifixion. But when Paul wrote Galatians, crucifixion was being practised. Not only was it a symbol of death but a very bloody and violent death at that, bringing with it total humiliation as the victim was hung on the cross stark naked to be exposed entirely before everybody.

A. W. Tozer wrote the following:

> *"The cross of Christ is the most revolutionary thing ever to appear among men. The cross of the Roman times knew no compromise; it never made concessions. It won all its arguments by killing its opponent and silencing him for good. It spared not Christ, by slew Him the same as the rest. He was alive when they hung Him on that cross and completely dead when they took him down six hours later. That was the cross the first time it appeared in Christian history. The cross effects its ends by destroying one established pattern, the victim's, and creating another pattern, its own. Thus it*

always has its way. It wins by defeating its opponent and imposing its will upon him. It always dominates. It never compromises, never dickers nor confers, never surrenders a point for the sake of peace. It cares not for peace; it cares only to end its opposition as fast as possible."

With perfect knowledge of all this Christ said:

Luke 9:23 (NIV) "If anyone would come after me, he must deny himself and take up his cross daily and follow me."[5]

This is what it means to pick up the cross and follow Him. Every day the Christian is to die and be humiliated. It's not a pleasant thought, but this is the reality of following Jesus. The call is to die each and every day to one's own will, desires and plans. To place everything at the foot of the cross and cry out, "Lord, take it all!" Each and every day to walk humbly, not with pride but to be humble.

But He gives a greater grace. Therefore it says, "God is opposed to the proud, but gives grace to the humble."

- James 4:6

God opposes the proud. If God seems somewhat distant from you, could you have a proud heart that might be causing Him to resist you? It may or may not be the case, only you will really know the answer to this for God can't walk with a proud person. Only those who are humble will know God.

He leads the humble in justice,
And He teaches the humble His way.
- Psalm 25:9

God makes His ways known to the humble in heart, not the

proud, self-assured person. If you are a Christian with pride, humble yourself before God. Otherwise, He will find a way to do it Himself; remember that it is much better for you if you do it yourself!

Pride will usually lead you to think yourself either better than other people or result in an unteachable spirit. Both are dangerous for the soul.

Most people who think they are better than other Christians usually are so because they despise the Church (*See Chapter Ten*). For whatever reason they have they believe that they have all the answers and that theirs is the only corner on truth. They then, of course, point a condemning finger at every other Christian.

Remember, the Bible declares all people sinners. You cannot accuse other Christians lest you are like the accuser (*Revelation 12:10*).

Now those with an unteachable spirit are in greater danger because being unteachable means you can never learn. No matter what anyone tells you, you are 'never wrong.' If someone tries to correct you, you will always ignore them completely.

A man who hardens his neck after much reproof
Will suddenly be broken beyond remedy.
- Proverbs 29:1

Refusing to accept rebukes is fatal – one who continually ignores any correction has a hard heart. Pride is the hardness! The only way God deals with proud people is to bring them down.

In the book of Esther in the Bible, there is a man called Haman. He was a very proud man and was made what would be the modern-day equivalent to the Prime Minister in the ancient Persian Empire. He plotted to destroy the Jewish people by tricking the king and even built a gallows by his house to kill Mordecai the Jew. Earlier Mordecai had discovered a plot to assassinate the king and thereby saved the king's life. The king remembers this just as Haman approaches him to ask him about hanging Mordecai on the gallows. The king asks Haman the best way to honour someone he delights to honour. Haman, thinking it to be himself, gives a very elaborate detail of the kind of reward he would like. The king's response?

> *Then the king said to Haman, "Take quickly the robes and the horse as you have said, and do so for Mordecai the Jew, who is sitting at the king's gate; do not fall short in anything of all that you have said."*
>
> *- Esther 6:10*

Haman was humiliated! Not only that, but his plot to exterminate the Jews was uncovered by Queen Esther herself and the king had him hung on the very gallows he had built for Mordecai! God is very often very ironic in His judgments (*Please see Revelation 16:4-7*).

> *He who digs a pit will fall into it,*
> *And he who rolls a stone, it will come back on him.*
>
> *- Proverbs 26:27*

You see, God rejects the proud but shows mercy to the humble. If you hold onto pride, you will create a wall between you and God. Pride is a deadly characteristic, avoid it at all costs. A proud person is essentially saying: "I don't need God! I can run my own life!" God especially despises and utterly detests it. The world might try and convince you that you need to be a proud person, but God is looking at the humble.

> *For consider your calling, brethren, that there were not many wise according to the flesh, not many mighty, not many noble; but God has chosen the foolish things of the world to shame the wise, and God has chosen the weak things of the world to shame the things which are strong, and the base things of the world and the despised God has chosen, the things that are not, so that He may nullify the things that are, so that no man may boast before God.*
>
> *- 1 Corinthians 1:26-29*

To pray:

"Father, forgive me for the pride of my heart. I know that it is written that You give Your grace to those who are humble. But for those who have pride, You resist. I don't want You to resist me, so please help me to have humility. To remember how small I am before You and yet despite this You still love me. I love You, so I will honour You with my ways. In Jesus' Name. Amen."

CHAPTER NINE: BESETTING SIN

The steps of a man are established by the Lord, and He delights in his way. When he falls, he will not be hurled headlong, because the Lord is the One who holds his hand.

Psalm 37:23-24

This book was first completed in 2015, after which, it received a significant amount of editing and refining. This chapter was the last one to have been written because it was the most challenging both to me personally and practically speaking. It is currently the end of October 2020 and I am revisiting it, as what was written before didn't work for me in my struggle against sin. I have learnt what really works for me to get victory and now I want to relay a few things. For one of the surest promises of God in the Bible is the power over the dominion of sin – that being the power over the sin in life.

Yet so many; even Christians, are bound by lusts and earthly desires. And they are growing more potent with a higher intensity as the days go by. This has to be one of the biggest reasons why people feel that God is distant from them. God is full of loving-kindness but He will certainly discipline and give a spanking to His people for their sin but only as a loving Father. Howbeit, His chastisement can be, and often is, severe. But they are always wounds of love that He inflicts (*Proverbs 27:6*). This is not to be confused with condemnation, which is **not** the Christian's portion.

> *But when we are judged, we are disciplined by the Lord so that we will not be condemned along with the world.*
> *- 1 Corinthians 11:32*

The point of this kind of chastisement is to bring the one receiving it closer to God. He doesn't beat you over the head about your sins, but He will do what He has to.

> *You have not yet resisted to the point of shedding blood in your striving against sin; and you have forgotten the exhortation which is addressed to you as sons,*
>
> *"My son, do not regard lightly the discipline of the Lord,*
> *Nor faint when you are reproved by Him;*
> *For those whom the Lord loves He disciplines,*
> *And He scourges every son whom He receives."*
> *- Hebrews 12:4-6*

> *Furthermore, we had earthly fathers to discipline us, and we respected them; shall we not much rather be subject to the Father of spirits, and live? For they disciplined us for a short time as seemed best to them, but He disciplines us for our good, so that we may share His holiness.*
> *- Hebrews 12:9-10*

If you are a sincere Christian and you truly love Jesus, but you've got a sin or a habit, something ungodly in your life, then God will deal with it. As a loving Father, yes, but He **will** deal with it.

However, only the honest Christian gets the mercy of God. It is a dangerous thing to play games with God. That is to wilfully sin, believing that one simply can because He is a God of grace and love. Be careful!

For if we go on sinning willfully after receiving the knowledge of the truth, there no longer remains a sacrifice for sins, but a terrifying expectation of judgment and the fury of a fire which will consume the adversaries.

- Hebrews 10:26-27

Sin cannot be overcome if the Holy Spirit is not present and working. Willpower alone will not be sufficient. I have tried so many times in my own willpower to say no to a besetting sin, but it proved futile. For willpower without the Holy Spirit's work within us is not enough to give us victory. That's why the Bible commands the believer to walk in the Spirit (*See Galatians 5:16*). This requires a person to recognise their need for God in the first place. To see themselves as they truly are: sick and in need of healing. Naturally this causes them to be broken in heart over their condition.

The Lord is near to the brokenhearted
And saves those who are crushed in spirit.

- Psalm 34:18

This verse is fascinating, but it is often overlooked. The words "broken" (from the Hebrew "shabar"[6]) and "crushed" (from the Hebrew "dakka"[7]) are sometimes thought by people to refer experiences less than drastic, but the Hebrew words used don't suggest that. "Shabar" is used to refer to situations of break down, breaking in pieces, collapse, shattering, smashing. "Dakka'" is used in relation to pulverizing (in Psalm 90.3 the word "dust" is "dakka").

What God is saying through David in Psalm 34 is a very profound thing. He is describing a heart that is so burdened down with such an incredible desire for God and a burden of failing Him that it is shattered because of the pressure of the weight of sin and guilt. He is talking about a person whose spirit is overwhelmed to the point of being so crushed it is like dust. These people are the ones that God comes to save. God wants a people who have a hatred for sin, not just sorrow at being found out. 2 Corinthians 7.8-11, especially verse 11 refers to godly sorrow producing earnestness, vindication, indignation, and zeal.

If you read Psalm 38, you get a perfect picture of how sin literally affects a Christian. Sin for a true Christian is a very heavy and unbearable load that is made so by God to drive them to the cross where they cast it away. This could be one of the reasons why Jesus said the following:

> *Take My yoke upon you and learn from Me, for I am gentle and humble in heart, and you will find rest for your souls. For My yoke is easy and My burden is light."*
>
> *- Matthew 11:29-30*

God makes sin so heavy that the Christian can stand it no longer and flees to the *easy* yoke and *light* burden of Jesus Christ as opposed to the terrible task master of sin. Do note, that those who do not belong to Jesus Christ cannot understand that sin is heavy. Only the true believer understands this.

Now sexual sin is a common problem among Christians today, and this problem is more widespread than we actually realise. This is because of the associated shame nobody is willing to talk about it publicly, lest they are considered strange.

I was in a meeting where the Spirit of God began to move. One of the young men started to open up publicly about how he was sexually abused years ago but which God had only recently freed him from. The preacher also opened up about a previous struggle with pornography that she had now overcome. The following week, near the end of the meeting droves of both men and women, were confessing to the sexual sin: masturbation, pornography, sexual immorality etc. that had gripped their lives. The people concerned were not only men but both men and women

(A crucial detail because it is wrongly assumed that it is just a male problem. Instead, this is a human problem. The nature of the issue being what it is, women are so much more reluctant to open up about it).

Folks, there is forgiveness and victory in Jesus Christ, but under no circumstances are you to give up fighting and to lie down with your sin justifying your condition. Some people would say otherwise. Listen to this solemn message from a well-known pastor in New York City:

> *"I read a sermon by a famous preacher here in New York given in an uptown cathedral. He said, "Don't suppress those deep feelings. Let go! Give yourself over to it, otherwise you'll destroy your personality." That preacher is going to face an army of damned souls in hell who won't let him rest for all eternity for lying to them!"* [8]

These are some strong words, but it is a very solemn warning. Unless there is a knowledge that something is a sin and a desire to depart from it is present one cannot possibly overcome it. How can you overcome anything if you don't believe it is wrong, and do not want to stop?

> *For the desire of the flesh is against the Spirit, and the Spirit against the flesh; for these are in opposition to one another, in order to keep you from doing whatever you want. But if you are led by the Spirit, you are not under the Law.*
>
> *- Galatians 5:17-18*

This is a fight that only the Christian – the truly born again person experiences. The man of the world knows nothing of this violent struggle. Since his spirit is dead (*Ephesians 2:1*), there is no struggle between spirit and flesh (the human nature). It's only the flesh that rules and reigns in his body. But the Christian has an inner war. How does one receive the victory?

Thanks be to God through Jesus Christ our Lord! *So then, on the one hand I myself with my mind am serving the law of God, but on the other, with my flesh the law of sin.*

- Romans 7:25 (Emphasis added)

It is Jesus Christ that delivers, but how is this so? Well, there is the inner working of the Holy Spirit. How does He, however, save from besetting sins?

They shall be My people, and I will be their God; and I will give them one heart and one way, that they may fear Me always, for their own good and for the good of their children after them. I will make an everlasting covenant with them that I will not turn away from them, to do them good; and I will put the fear of Me in their hearts so that they will not turn away from Me.

- Jeremiah 32:38-40

Why does the struggle go on for so long? One of the reasons is a lack of the fear of God. It is reverence for God, but this fear of God is more than just that. The word for fear in Hebrew is yir'â[6], which means fear, morally reverence: - dreadful, exceedingly, fear, fearful. This implies that the fear of God contains a considerable amount of dread with it. Many Christians say that the fear of God is only respect for God, it has nothing to do with dread of God or being afraid of Him. Yet this interpretation cannot be true because Jesus Himself links the fear of God directly with hell:

"I say to you, My friends, do not be afraid of those who kill the body and after that have no more that they can do. But I will warn you whom to fear: ***fear the One who, after He has killed, has authority to cast into hell; yes, I tell you, fear Him!***

- Luke 12:4-5 (Emphasis added)

Also, consider the following:

And so terrible was the sight, that Moses said, "I am full of fear and trembling." But you have come to Mount Zion and to the city of the living God, the heavenly Jerusalem, and to myriads of angels, to the general assembly and church of the firstborn who are enrolled in heaven, and to God, the Judge of all, and to the spirits of the righteous made perfect, and to Jesus, the mediator of a new covenant, and to the sprinkled blood, which speaks better than the blood of Abel. See to it that you do not refuse Him who is speaking. For if those did not escape when they refused him who warned them on earth, much less will we escape who turn away from Him who warns from heaven?

- Hebrews 12:21-25

The fear of God is a good place to start. It leads a person to flee to Christ for mercy and keeps them going back to Him every time they do fall.

By lovingkindness and truth iniquity is atoned for,
And by the fear of the Lord one keeps away from evil.

- Proverbs 16:6

In order for there to be victory, the first thing someone needs is a willingness to bring it to the light, that is to bring it out in the open before God and possibly before another person. This requires honesty and courage. You will never have victory if you hide your sin.

This is the judgment, that the Light has come into the world, and men loved the darkness rather than the Light, for their deeds were evil. For everyone who does evil hates the Light, and does not come to the Light for fear that his deeds will be exposed. But he who practices the truth comes to the Light, so that his deeds may be manifested as having been wrought in God."

- John 3:19-21

If you read Genesis 3, you will notice that the first thing Adam and Eve did after they sinned was to hide from God. They feared, but it was a fear that caused them to run away. A human response that is rather unhelpful, for there is no help away from God.

This is perhaps one of the reasons that people are atheist. In my experience, when someone claims adamantly that there is no God, they are very often sexually immoral or promiscuous. You can argue that point all you want, but I stand by this as being my experience. In my own life, I was wilfully engaging in a particular sin; one that I thought I could hide from people. At this time, I thought it was kept secret. It was, just only from the people around me. That very evening during a prayer meeting, a word was given. The person giving the word didn't know who it was for but spoke it out to all who were present. It was as follows:

"God can see what you are doing in the dark."

Hiding sin does us no good. I was terribly afraid because I felt as if in my inner man I could see God upon His throne in heaven staring right at me as I was creeping around in my sin. Yet this in and of itself did not give me the power to overcome it. Just before the COVID-19 lockdown in the UK (literally the last Sunday that we gathered before we had a national lockdown), I had a meeting with my Pastor and told him about all my sin and journey into it without holding back. He was very loving and gracious towards me and gave me some advice. A willingness to bring it to the light so that it can be dealt with is so important. That is why accountability is such a good thing, for we often need the support and encouragement from other believers.

Christians may also have different kinds of temptations and inclinations in the types of sins that they are drawn towards. Some bring a great deal of shame to those who are experiencing them. Yet Jesus Christ is not ashamed of you in whatever struggle or temptation is your weak spot. He has a great deal of love for you and is able to understand you.

> *For we do not have a high priest who cannot sympathize with our weaknesses, but One who has been tempted in all things as we are, yet without sin.*
>
> *- Hebrews 4:15*

So firstly you need the fear of God that drives you to Christ. And this is essential because it also maintains the Christian's life.

If you address as Father the One who impartially judges according to each one's work, conduct yourselves in fear during the time of your stay on earth.

- 1 Peter 1:17

The great danger of sin is that the heart can become so hardened, that rather than returning to Christ and allowing Him to deal with it, that the person will not give it up. Either that or the person will be in a terrible state of despair in a merry-go-round of sin, confess, sin, confess.

"And although they say, 'As the Lord lives,'
Surely they swear falsely."
O Lord, do not Your eyes look for truth?
You have smitten them,
But they did not weaken;
You have consumed them,
But they refused to take correction.
They have made their faces harder than rock;
They have refused to repent.

- Jeremiah 5:2-3

These are people; possibly even people who profess to be believers, who are so in love with their sins that they literally give themselves over to them. This might result in their leaving the faith, or to still professing the Name of Christ whilst justifying their practices by either distorting biblical truth or flatly ignoring it. A claim is made to know God but they cannot be told that their lifestyle is wrong as they have hardened themselves against the truth, despite whatever their claim on Christ is. And any attempt to correct them would only result in their being unable to see that it is indeed wrong, despite whatever bible proof you could give them.

> *To the pure, all things are pure; but to those who are defiled and unbelieving, nothing is pure, but both their mind and their conscience are defiled. They profess to know God, but by their deeds they deny Him, being detestable and disobedient and worthless for any good deed.*
>
> *- Titus 1:15-16*

I heard a testimony from a Christian young lady who told of a story of how she was with her friend once and was suddenly overcome with lesbian desires towards her friend. She fought (according to her) against these lesbian feelings. After a while, she was at Church one time wrestling with what she described as these homosexual desires. She was trying to figure out if it was, in fact, God's will for her to be a lesbian. She decided during the worship to give her all to God during worship, and, as she put it, was overcome with a sense of release, peace and freedom from a burden. That God had given her an assurance of her lesbianism.

Actually, God was really convicting her of her sin of lusting after other girls because she was not fighting against sin and resisting it as a Christian ought to. A Christian may have a struggle, but he or she will fight. Yet really the reality was that she was fighting with God and His conviction. In her life she loved her lesbianism and was unwilling to depart from it, she was seeking for God's approval on her lifestyle and therefore resisted His 'No'. In the end, God removed His restraining hand so that she was given up by God to her sin: *'If you will not listen to Me, then go and do what you really want. I will not stop you.'*

This is often a judgement of God that He does when He knows that the person concerned loves their sin so much that they will never ever repent. He withdraws from them and allows them to do what they want with a false sense of peace. Normally, when this happens, it means that there is no way back for them, because repentance is a gift given to us by God (*Acts 11:18 & 2 Timothy 2:25*). Like all gifts, it can be withdrawn (*Hebrews 6:6*). The preachers of old used to call this, 'Sinning away the day of grace.'

Where God strives with a person no more, letting them go their own way, into eternal destruction. If you are still feeling convicted for your sin, that God is troubling you for it, thank God for it. As much as you don't feel it, that is incredibly great news. That means there is hope for you yet because God has not given up on you! He is still fighting for you.

Sin is so severe that Jesus said that one ought to go to extraordinary lengths to get rid of it.

If your hand causes you to stumble, cut it off; it is better for you to enter life crippled, than, having your two hands, to go into hell, into the unquenchable fire, [where their worm does not die, and the fire is not quenched.] If your foot causes you to stumble, cut it off; it is better for you to enter life lame, than, having your two feet, to be cast into hell, [where their worm does not die, and the fire is not quenched.] If your eye causes you to stumble, throw it out; it is better for you to enter the kingdom of God with one eye, than, having two eyes, to be cast into hell, where their worm does not die, and the fire is not quenched.

- Mark 9:43-48

Obviously, Jesus is not talking about self-mutilation. What Jesus is saying here is that if there is anything in your life that is a temptation for you and causes you to sin – cut it out of your life if you have to. It is better to lack something than to go to hell. This is what Jesus is saying.

What you have to understand, is that all sin begins in the mind. That is where the fight is.

for the weapons of our warfare are not of the flesh, but divinely powerful for the destruction of fortresses. We are destroying speculations and every lofty thing raised up against the knowledge of God, and we are taking every thought captive to the obedience of Christ.

- 2 Corinthians 10:4-5

The enemy's main strategy to bring a believer into bondage and sin is through lies. They are normally lies about God Himself.

> *'God is not providing for your needs and cravings,
> so here is my solution instead!'*

An example of that would be, *'God has not provided a husband or wife for your sexual needs, here is masturbation.'* This may not be your struggle but for you it might be something else. Each person faces a temptation uniquely designed for them by satan corresponding to their weakness. Everyone has different struggles but the same principle applies to all. This is why faith is a shield (*Ephesians 6:16*). Faith not only in Jesus for salvation but also faith in God's character. Faith that He knows your weakness, He understands your needs and will provide for them all. Exercising faith in God's care as Father is essential to victory. Reading the promises of God out loud is a good way to go and has proved helpful to me. If satan can make you doubt that God is good you are already as good as fallen.

This leads on nicely to the next point in which the only way to truly overcome is to fully surrender to Jesus Christ every area of your life. This is what I know from experience is one of the only ways I know how to live in constant victory. This is because idolatry is a very big stumbling block leading to sin and no lukewarm Christian ever triumphed in anything for God. Ever!

> *"Son of man, these men have set up their idols in their hearts and have put right before their faces the stumbling block of their iniquity. Should I be consulted by them at all? Therefore speak to them and tell them, 'Thus says the Lord God, "Any man of the house of Israel who sets up his idols in his heart, puts right before his face the stumbling block of his iniquity, and then comes to the prophet, I the Lord will be brought to give him an answer in the matter in view of the multitude of his idols, in order to lay hold of the hearts of the house of Israel who are estranged from Me through all their idols."'*
>
> *"Therefore say to the house of Israel, 'Thus says the Lord God,*

> *"Repent and turn away from your idols and turn your faces away from all your abominations.*
>
> *- Ezekiel 14:3-6*

The idols themselves were the stumbling blocks. This passage suggests that idols in the heart of the believer will always lead them astray and that God refuses to speak to people who have idols in their hearts until they repent. It also mentions being estranged from God due to idols which can be a reason why God seems to be distant.

So a full surrender to the Lordship of Jesus Christ is needed. No stone unturned, no relationship that He hasn't ordained in your life, no pleasure or precious thing that He hasn't given you permission for. That means He has total and unchallenged control over all the affairs of your life. It's one thing on Sunday to sing 'All to Jesus I surrender,' but it is quite another thing to actually live it! Above all, remember that God is holy and will judge sin. He will not overlook it, even in His own people, for sin **will** have consequences (*Galatians 6:7-8*).

> *For it is time for judgment to begin with the household of God; and if it begins with us first, what will be the outcome for those who do not obey the gospel of God? And if it is with difficulty that the righteous is saved, what will become of the godless man and the sinner?*
>
> *- 1 Peter 4:17-18*

The point of the matter is this, if you have a sin in your life, lay it down. The love of God and all that God has for us on the other side of eternity far outweighs any momentary pleasure you have down here on earth.

To pray:

"Father, I acknowledge my sin to You. You say that if I confess my sin, then you will be faithful and just to forgive me of my sin. "I am so sick and tired of constantly committing this sin. But I

will trust You to deliver me from this sin. I love You, and I want this thing out of my life for good. Help me to fight with all my heart and to live a clean, pure and holy life. You sent Your Son to die on the cross for my freedom. I don't want Him to have died in vain. Now I want to lay my sin down and walk with You more fully, I want no walls between us. In Jesus' Name. Amen.

CHAPTER TEN: LOVE THE BRIDE

"Who is this coming up from the wilderness leaning on her beloved?"

Song of Solomon 8:5

It is essential for a Christian to love the bride. One must love the Church to be part of this body of believers.

> *For I am jealous for you with a godly jealousy; for I betrothed you to one husband, so that to Christ I might present you as a pure virgin.*
>
> *- 2 Corinthians 11:2*

Paul was writing to the Church in Corinth, but the implications go beyond just that Church in that time. When the Israelites were chosen by God to be His special people, His covenant relationship with them as a people was to be one of intimacy in which He called Himself the Husband and Israel His wife. God compared Israel's idolatry to adultery.

God says, "If a husband divorces his wife
And she goes from him

> *And belongs to another man,*
> *Will he still return to her?*
> *Will not that land be completely polluted?*
> *But you are a harlot with many lovers;*
> *Yet you turn to Me," declares the Lord.*
>
> *- Jeremiah 3:1*

The people of Israel had a very rocky relationship with God, to say the least. The Bible actually states that unless God had specifically spared Israel due to His promise with their forefather Abraham, they would have been destroyed just like Sodom and Gomorrah (*Isaiah 1:9*). Israel had a history of continual idolatry and turning away from God that eventually brought with it a judgement that caused them to be carried off to other lands. God actually stopped being Israel's husband (*However please see Psalm 105:8-11 & Jeremiah 31:31-37*), when Assyria came and took Israel away captive.

> *And I saw that for all the adulteries of faithless Israel, I had sent her away and given her a writ of divorce, yet her treacherous sister Judah did not fear; but she went and was a harlot also.*
>
> *- Jeremiah 3:8*

A husband and wife relationship is to be a type of Christ's relationship with His Church. That's what the whole purpose of marriage is supposed to be: a mirror that reflects Christ and His people.

That kind of intimacy between husband and wife is to be a picture of that closeness and love between Christ and His Church. It's very crucial that Christians have a right attitude towards the Church, one of proper respect. How the Church is viewed is one way to tell if somebody really belongs to God in the first place.

> *Whoever believes that Jesus is the Christ is born of God, and whoever loves the Father loves the child born of Him.*
>
> *- 1 John 5:1*

In other words, whoever loves God loves His people, the Church, which is the children of God – those who are born of God. If you love God, you will love His Church. There are many Christians who loudly raise their voices against the Church of Jesus Christ. There are also many believers that claim that they just don't 'do Church.' One of the ways to tell whether or not one is truly saved is by the love for other Christians.

> *Do not be surprised, brethren, if the world hates you. We know that we have passed out of death into life, because we love the brethren. He who does not love abides in death.*
>
> *- 1 John 3:13-14*

Here John says that one can be assured of eternal life because of love for other Christians, even more so, it explicitly states that the world hates the Church. If you despise the Church of Christ, then you and the world are of the same spirit. Jesus said that the world loves its own (*See John 15:19*).

Do not think to raise your fist against the bride because she does have a Beloved, so before you think of bringing '*correction*' to her ask yourself something. Do you want to because you love the Church and want to help her? Or is it because you hate the Church and love the world?

> *We love, because He first loved us. If someone says, "I love God," and hates his brother, he is a liar; for the one who does not love his brother whom he has seen, cannot love God whom he has not seen. And this commandment we have from Him, that the one who loves God should love his brother also.*
>
> *- 1 John 4:19-21*

A man can't claim to love God and hate other Christians. It's impossible. The Bible commands that Christians ought to love one another with sincerity from the heart.

> *Since you have in obedience to the truth purified your souls for a*

> *sincere love of the brethren, fervently love one another from the heart.*
>
> *- 1 Peter 1:22*

God pours His love into the hearts of believers, and they start loving one another, which brings a beautiful unity, being one body even though they are many. Remember how God said of mankind at Babel *'nothing which they purpose to do will be impossible for them (Genesis 11:6).'* God said nothing was impossible for them because they all had one language and one common goal – which, of course, was to build a tower. If Christians live in unity with one another, then nothing shall be impossible for them also. Jesus promised that if His people gather in His name and ask for anything from God, then it will be done for them (*See Matthew 18:19-20*).

There is also another reason why it's essential that Christians live in harmony with one another. When He was in the garden of Gethsemane, Jesus prayed to His Father that His people would be in unity with one another.

> *"I do not ask on behalf of these alone, but for those also who believe in Me through their word; that they may all be one; even as You, Father, are in Me and I in You, that they also may be in Us, so that the world may believe that You sent Me.*
>
> *- John 17:20-21*

It does no good for God's Kingdom when 'Christians' attack the Church. It doesn't glorify God at all. Your overall attitude to the Church and fellow Christians will show you what kind of heart you have. If you despise the Church – it will be mainly for two reasons. You will both be full of pride and think you are better than every other Christian or you will be living with and harbouring a secret sin that the Church openly condemns.

There may be some of you who are neither harbouring a secret sin nor are full of pride but instead have been severely wounded by Christians. This is such a sorry situation, but you shouldn't be angry at God or with the Church for what has happened to you because of these hypocrites. There is a true Church, and there are phonies. Those who abused you in such an office will answer to God for their crimes, but you need to forgive them for your sake (*Please see Chapter Six*). You won't be able to move on if you don't forgive them. Don't blame the Church for something that someone did to you, it will probably be the case that the person concerned, despite whatever walk with God they claim to have is actually not a real Christian in the first place.

Don't hate the Church. Be careful because the Church belongs to Jesus. She is His Church. So she must be treated with respect and honour.

To pray:

"Father, please forgive me for the wrong attitude towards Your Church and towards other Christians. Help me to love and respect other believers. Deliver me from all wrong attitudes and motives in the way I interact with the Church. I love You, and I will love Your people also. In Jesus' Name. Amen."

CHAPTER ELEVEN: GETTING OVER THE 'CROWD EFFECT'

But the one who endures to the end, he will be saved.

Matthew 24:13

The title is a little unusual, but the meaning behind it is straightforward. For example, you go away to a Christian retreat or something like that, and you get spiritually hyped up with the crowd of people who are with you and become excited about God only to discover afterwards that the feeling has gone away. Perhaps you have experienced this and wondered where your faith has gone.

There are countless numbers of young people leaving the Church in droves. They went to a week away or a retreat of some kind and had their faith revived so to speak. They last a few weeks but their overall result is like fireworks - a loud bang and lots of noise, but then it dies!

Now to Him who is able to keep you from stumbling, *and to make you stand in the presence of His glory blameless with great*

> *joy, to the only God our Savior, through Jesus Christ our Lord, be glory, majesty, dominion and authority, before all time and now and forever. Amen.*
>
> *- Jude 24 (Emphasis added)*

God, through the indwelling Holy Spirit, has the power to keep the Christian from falling away from Him. This passage from the book of Jude confirms this. So why are so many turning away from God and falling away? If God has the power to keep people, then why aren't they being kept? The fault as always does not lie with God but the person concerned.

> *But the Spirit explicitly says that in later times some will fall away from the faith, paying attention to deceitful spirits and doctrines of demons, by means of the hypocrisy of liars seared in their own conscience as with a branding iron.*
>
> *- 1 Timothy 4:1-2*

These are the last days; these are the later times that the Bible is describing. Even today in plain sight of all, many false teachers can be seen arising from all over the place bringing with them heresies into the Church. They are ministers of satan masquerading as ministers of Christ and ultimately promoting that which God is against, often twisting the Bible to do so.

> *The grass withers, the flower fades,*
> *But the word of our God stands forever.*
>
> *- Isaiah 40:8*

Why is this deception so sweeping amongst vast multitudes of professing Christians?

> *For the time will come when they will not endure sound doctrine; but wanting to have their ears tickled, they will accumulate for themselves teachers in accordance to their own desires, and will turn away their ears from the truth and will turn aside to myths.*
>
> *- 2 Timothy 4:3-4*

This is talking about those who go to Church not to hear what God has to say but to be told what they want to hear.

Who say to the seers, "You must not see visions";
And to the prophets, "You must not prophesy to us what is right,
Speak to us pleasant words,
Prophesy illusions.
"Get out of the way, turn aside from the path,
Let us hear no more about the Holy One of Israel."
- Isaiah 30:10-11

You can see that this is precisely what is happening today. Some people want to hear a lot about how much God loves them and wants to bless them (which is actually true). Yet at the same time, they really don't want to hear about holiness and the need to live a moral and pure life before God. You cannot live as you please in sin and then expect to go to heaven. This is a hard truth to hear, but it is precisely that, the truth!

You need to see the exceeding sinfulness of your sin before you can truly appreciate the grace and mercy of God. If you understand how terrible your sins are in the sight of God, you are more likely to leave them. And you'll get over the 'crowd' effect too.

No doubt you know of the parable of the sower (*See Matthew 13:1-8*). There was a sower who went out and scattered seed in his field. Some fell on the path and was eaten by birds. Some fell on rocky places and grew up quickly but also withered just as soon as it had no root and the sun had caused it to wither. Some fell amongst thorns where it was choked. Only the seed that fell on good soil flourished.

"Hear then the parable of the sower. When anyone hears the word of the kingdom and does not understand it, the evil one comes and snatches away what has been sown in his heart. This is the one on whom seed was sown beside the road.

- Matthew 13:18-19

The majority of mankind fits into this category. Before God's message has a chance to take root in their hearts, satan comes immediately, and they harden their hearts against the word. This is because they have given up a place for the devil in their lives. Sadly it may even be that you will read all this and altogether reject what is being said to you. This is because you allow the devil to pluck the word out of your heart.

The one on whom seed was sown on the rocky places, this is the man who hears the word and immediately receives it with joy; yet he has no firm root in himself, but is only temporary, and when affliction or persecution arises because of the word, immediately he falls away.

- Matthew 13:20-21

Such a person has no root. This is the key to this entire chapter. They have no root and so, therefore, are unfruitful in their lives.

Abide in Me, and I in you. As the branch cannot bear fruit of itself unless it abides in the vine, so neither can you unless you abide in Me. I am the vine, you are the branches; he who abides in Me and I in him, he bears much fruit, for apart from Me you can do nothing.

- John 15:4-5

Jesus has to live in the believer. This seed managed to do a little well on its own, but it didn't last. In the same way, some may go a little while in the Christian life without Jesus, but eventually, they will run out of steam. And that's what happened to many of you too, as you came back from these kinds of Christian retreats.

These kinds of people, for whatever reason, thought that the Christian life would bring success and fulfilment. They didn't realise that being a Christian would bring them trouble, persecution and suffering for Jesus' sake.

> *And the one on whom seed was sown among the thorns, this is the man who hears the word, and the worry of the world and the deceitfulness of wealth choke the word, and it becomes unfruitful.*
>
> *- Matthew 13:22*

The world has gotten in the way of this person. The pleasures of this world stamp out any work of God in their lives.

> *By faith Moses, when he had grown up, refused to be called the son of Pharaoh's daughter, choosing rather to endure ill-treatment with the people of God than to enjoy the passing pleasures of sin, considering the reproach of Christ greater riches than the treasures of Egypt; for he was looking to the reward.*
>
> *- Hebrews 11:24-26*

You can't have Jesus and the world. Jesus Himself said in Matthew 6:24 that we can't have two masters. If we try to have the world and Jesus, then this world will choke out our fruit and our love for Jesus. It is a dangerous game to play to jump from Church to nightclubs, for example. Some of you reading this are in this category. You've allowed the things of this world to take you away from Jesus. Stop loving the world and stop playing games with God. If you don't quit fooling around with these things, then they will be the death of you.

> *And the one on whom seed was sown on the good soil, this is the man who hears the word and understands it; who indeed bears fruit and brings forth, some a hundredfold, some sixty, and some thirty."*
>
> *- Matthew 13:23*

This is where one should desire to be. And this is what it comes down to. You see, a week away somewhere receiving a spiritual high won't do anything for you if you have nothing going on inside of you. If the life of God isn't within you, you will burn out and run dry. Your love for Jesus will grow cold, and your life will return to how it was before your spiritual experience.

The problem in the time of Jesus was that the Pharisees wanted a Saviour to deliver them from the hands of the Romans. The Jews were all looking for a conquering King who would take care of all their problems straight away. Many who come to Christ expect Him to make everything alright. Kind of like how you may have gone to one of these weeks away got hyped up on God and expected everything to change when you arrived home. But God doesn't work that way. When Jesus came to the Jews, it was to deal with the heart issue of sin – He was on His way to the cross to die for the sins of the world. Right now, God's more interested in the condition of your heart than how great your life is.

God changes hearts. If outside of camp you have no time for God, then don't expect your life to change. If God isn't doing a work inside of you, then any 'love for God' you have will soon empty. The crowd effect you receive is just an emotional high and nothing more. If it isn't grounded in a relationship with Jesus, then the experience was nothing more than just a delightful experience. It carries with it no eternal significance.

> *"Not everyone who says to Me, 'Lord, Lord,' will enter the kingdom of heaven, but he who does the will of My Father who is in heaven will enter.*
>
> *- Matthew 7:21*

Not everyone who claims to be Christian is actually a Christian. If your commitment to Jesus is limited to that one week away, then you are not a Christian. If your commitment to Jesus is limited to Sunday while at Church, then you are not a Christian. Just because you prayed that one time doesn't mean you are going to heaven. It is hard to hear, but this is a truth that is so important that it must be plainly stated.

So in all of this, how does one resolve the problem. If you made it this far, you very well must have an open heart. Are you earnestly interested in finding out how to stay strong? For you see, it is entirely possible for a Christian to remain steady in his relationship with God without going up and down, in and out, hot and cold. It is accessed by faith as it is in reality, dependent upon the work of God rather than the emotional condition of the individual concerned. If you read Jeremiah 31:31-34 you will see that God intends to change the heart of the person, and this will lead to a definite difference in their behaviour. For you are given the Holy Spirit at your conversion. When you have Him living inside of you, He will begin to work. This is how the Holy Spirit keeps. It is not about you or how great you are or what kind of meeting you had with the crowd that is going to impact your life. It is about the Spirit of God moving in your life. You need to turn to Him and yield yourself to Him. Yield yourself to the process of being changed. Call on Him and ask Him to do it, which is if you genuinely are interested in following Him. He not only keeps, but He keeps until the very end.

> *He who overcomes will thus be clothed in white garments; and I will not erase his name from the book of life, and I will confess his name before My Father and before His angels.*
>
> *- Revelation 3:5*

To pray:

> *"Father, I recognise that I have relied too much on my feelings and that my faith has been put on my emotions. Your truth is solid whether or not my feelings line up with it. Forgive me, Lord. I will put all my trust in You. I ask You now Holy Spirit to come into my life and work in me so that You may change my life. Thank You for willing to work in me. I will walk by faith and not by what I can see or feel. In Jesus' Name. Amen."*

CHAPTER TWELVE: SUFFERING

"He delivers the afflicted in their affliction, and opens their ear in time of oppression.

Job 36:15

This subject is a very touchy subject for many people. God's distance never seems as high as when people are in great pain. Patience and a lot of love are needed for those who are suffering. The Bible says that Jesus Christ suffered, not just on the cross, but throughout His entire earthly life.

> *Although He was a Son, He learned obedience from the things which He suffered.*
>
> *- Hebrews 5:8*

He can sympathise with people in their pain. Do you remember reading Job and how useless his comforters were in consoling him?

> *"I have heard many such things;*
> *Sorry comforters are you all.*

- Job 16:2

People in pain don't want quotes from the Bible; they want people in pain who can understand their hurt. There is today so much suffering in the body of Jesus Christ. So many broken homes, hurting families, wrecked marriages etc. This chapter is a message of hope and consolation.

When you as a Christian suffer pain, usually you will either go off in one of two directions. Either in your sorrow, you will draw closer to Jesus, or you will get bitter and resentful towards God. Possibly the worst thing about suffering is not only the problem itself but the thousands of voices from hell itself that rise against you.

"God was going to keep you? See how that worked out!"

"You've prayed for years for your family, and there doesn't even seem to be one shred of hope of an answer to prayer."

"If God was all loving, why did He allow this to happen?"

The Bible gives a word of encouragement that there is a High Priest Who has a great deal of sympathy for the pain of people (*Hebrews 4:15*). God is not mad at you, blaming Him for your pain, but you need to take it to Him.

There is a notorious false doctrine going around that is something like this:

'We Christians are to be blessed – we are not called to suffer but to have the best things of life. If you are suffering it is because you don't have enough faith or you have a sin in your life.'

We are blessed, this is true, yet this is not always the case. In the Bible there are many wicked people who are blessed, so God's blessing does not always mean He approves of those He blesses (*See Matthew 5:45 & Romans 2:4*). People who are going through pain do not need someone else pouring condemnation on them to add to their burden. I know of a Christian who had an older brother with Schizophrenia. They went to Church, where the older brother gave his life to Jesus in the limited understanding that his mind had. Yet there was another believer who challenged the Christian with a rebuke, "Why wasn't your brother brought to the Church earlier so he could receive healing?" Being hurt by this comment, he left it with God. The believer who had been so condemning later had a son who was diagnosed with the very same illness Schizophrenia. One could argue it is an ironic coincidence, but I will not dare to presume so. Learn from this and do not attack someone in their suffering! Healing does belong to the children of God, but the attitude towards those who suffer should be one of love and gentleness.

Suffering As A Result Of Consequences For Sin

Suffering from sin happens all across the world. Prisons, for instance, all full of suffering people. If you are being afflicted because you are a lazy worker or because you cheat or steal, then really you need to accept the consequences of your actions. God is gracious and can forgive your mistakes, but you may have to face and even live with what you have done. As an example, consider the following:

> ***Why have you despised the word of the Lord by doing evil in His sight? You have struck down Uriah the Hittite with the sword, have taken his wife to be your wife, and have killed him with the sword of the sons of Ammon. Now, therefore, the sword shall never depart from your house, because you have despised Me and have taken the wife of Uriah the Hittite to be your wife.' Thus says the Lord, 'Behold, I will raise up evil against you from your own household; I will even take your wives before your eyes and give them to your companion, and he will lie with your wives in broad daylight.*** *Indeed you did it secretly, but I will do this thing before all Israel, and under the sun.'"* Then

*David said to Nathan, "I have sinned against the Lord." And Nathan said to David, "**The Lord also has taken away your sin; you shall not die**. However, because by this deed you have given occasion to the enemies of the Lord to blaspheme, **the child also that is born to you shall surely die**."*

- 2 Samuel 12:9-14 (Emphasis added)

As a result of his sin, David suffered in various means. It is true that God forgave him, no questions asked. Yet his sin brought upon him terrible consequences. Please see 2 Samuel 13:1-21, 2 Samuel 13:28-29, 2 Samuel 15:13-14, 2 Samuel 15:30, 2 Samuel 16:22 and 2 Samuel 19:4 for some of the fulfilments of what was said to David here.

There was a young man I heard about who was hooked on drugs. He was on his way to Dartford and fell asleep on the train when he woke up in Chatham. Desperate for a fix, he was sent to a medical practice which at the time was run by a Church. Once there, he received prayer where he gave his life to the Lord and was instantly set free from drug addiction. Eighteen months later, he died from AIDS. He was forgiven by God; he received the Holy Spirit and had that newness of life that Paul writes about in his letters. Yet God did not save him from this kind of suffering. He simply reaped the consequences of his drug abuse.

God does forgive and heal, but sometimes people have to live with their mistakes and their bad choices. If you have pain that is caused by your own stupid errors, God will not always remove the consequences to those mistakes, but He will give you the grace and the strength to endure it just as He did for David.

Suffering For Righteousness

If you love Jesus and you seek Him, you have already made an enemy. The moment you set your heart on seeking God with all that you have, it is then that the devil is going to mark you. You will have demons harassing you in various forms - but remember this:

You are from God, little children, and have overcome them; **because greater is He who is in you than he who is in the world.**

- 1 John 4:4 (Emphasis added)

Once you determine to go all the way with Jesus, you are going to become a target of the devil. This is a certainty. If he sees you as a threat to him or his kingdom, then he will aim his gun at you. However, he will equally leave you alone if he sees that you are not a threat.

"If the world hates you, you know that it has hated Me before it hated you. If you were of the world, the world would love its own; but because you are not of the world, but I chose you out of the world, because of this the world hates you.

- John 15:18-19

The Bible says that the world is under the sway of the wicked one (*1 John 5:19*). Their hatred towards God is going to be directed at His people. Now that particular harassment is going to come in various ways. You will have some people that will for no reason just hate you. They will simply hate you because the devil in them hates you for being a Christian. It's as simple as that. The devil hates you because of who you are in Christ.

Other times it will be more subtle than that. People will treat you as if you are foolish and ignorant. They will make the worst and most crude jokes just because you are in the room. Other times, you can be bullied and even isolated by members of your own family because of your faith.

and a man's enemies will be the members of his household.

- Matthew 10:36

If you thought that serving Jesus would cause you to enter into good company, then you are sadly mistaken. It is a very lonely path for those who walk with God. All of God's men have been lonely men. You will have fellow believers to encourage you, but there will be many times when it is just you and Jesus – nobody else is around.

It is impossible to escape suffering for Jesus' sake as it is written: *'Indeed, all who desire to live godly in Christ Jesus will be persecuted'* (*2 Timothy 3:12*). It is unavoidable; however, please consider the following:

> *"Therefore everyone who confesses Me before men, I will also confess him before My Father who is in heaven. But whoever denies Me before men, I will also deny him before My Father who is in heaven.*
>
> *- Matthew 10:32-33*

God sees everything, and He will reward you. Undoubtedly the most significant reward a Christian can ever receive when he or she gets to heaven is not the mansions, the golden harps, the angelic choirs, the crowns, etc. The greatest reward that a Christian can ever receive is to be recognised by God and for Him to turn and say about them: "This is my friend!" There can be no greater honour to ever be bestowed upon a human being.

If you suffer for Him and endure it patiently, that is what you will be to Him. Yes, fires of testing and persecution will come if they haven't already. But stand firm and know that God has not and will not forget you!

> *But Zion said, "The Lord has forsaken me,*
> *And the Lord has forgotten me."*
> *"Can a woman forget her nursing child*
> *And have no compassion on the son of her womb?*
> *Even these may forget, but I will not forget you.*
> *"Behold, I have inscribed you on the palms of My hands;*
> *Your walls are continually before Me.*
>
> *- Isaiah 49:14-16*

What do you think the inscribing on His hands are other than the wounds of the crucifixion nails?

However badly you are being treated by people for the Gospel, you must always pray for them and consider the following.

> *For you have been called for this purpose, since Christ also suffered for you, leaving you an example for you to follow in His steps, who committed no sin, nor was any deceit found in His mouth; and while being reviled, He did not revile in return; while suffering, He uttered no threats, but kept entrusting Himself to Him who judges righteously.*
>
> *- 1 Peter 2:21-23*

It is inconceivable that a Christian should be unwilling to suffer for His name. He suffered on the cross to set His people free from the power of satan, from the dominion of sin and from the wrath of Almighty God in the everlasting fires of hell. Surely, one can suffer a little for Him in this life. When the Christian is mistreated, they must not do likewise in response. There is an unseen spiritual war going on. The Church is fighting **for** all people, **not against** all people. These poor people who persecute the Church are under the power of the devil. That is what she fights against. She commits these people into God's hands that He may open their eyes. The enemy is the devil and his demons – not human beings who are created in the image of God.

> *Do not fear what you are about to suffer. Behold, the devil is about to cast some of you into prison, so that you will be tested, and you will have tribulation for ten days. Be faithful until death, and I will give you the crown of life.*
>
> *- Revelation 2:10*

Suffering Due To The Sin Of Others

This kind of suffering is one of the hardest to write about, mainly because the person who experiences this wrong has been subject to pain by the hand of another.

Recorded in the Bible is the story of someone who suffered at the hands of another – that man was Uriah the Hittite. The Bible actually records him in 1 Chronicles 11:41 as one of David's mighty men. Not only was Uriah faithful to God but was also fiercely loyal to David – being one of those mighty men. Yet David betrayed this man by taking advantage of Uriah's wife while he fought in the army and slept with her – which was just mentioned a moment ago. When she became pregnant, he sought to cover his sin up – when nothing he tried worked, he sent Uriah to his death.

> *Now in the morning David wrote a letter to Joab and sent it by the hand of Uriah. He had written in the letter, saying, "Place Uriah in the front line of the fiercest battle and withdraw from him, so that he may be struck down and die." So it was as Joab kept watch on the city, that he put Uriah at the place where he knew there were valiant men. The men of the city went out and fought against Joab, and some of the people among David's servants fell; and Uriah the Hittite also died.*
>
> *- 2 Samuel 11:14-17*

Uriah suffered, and yet the worst thing was that up to his death, he didn't know it. Another man impregnated his wife and had him killed. Uriah suffered cruelly at the hands of David because of his greed and lust. David thought that he had gotten away with it until Nathan, the prophet, pointed a finger in his face and said: "*You are the man!*" (*2 Samuel 12:7*).

Many times in your life, other people will sin against you in various ways, and they will significantly afflict and torment your souls by their hurtful and hateful actions. God always takes note of such incidences. You must not assume that God is going to strike them down straight away with a word of rebuke as He did for David. Yet keep in mind that God is always watching. God's silence does not mean He is unaware of what wicked people are doing (*See Psalm 50:16-21*). He will repay.

> *For we know Him who said, "Vengeance is Mine, I will repay." And again, "The Lord will judge His people." It is a terrifying thing to fall into the hands of the living God.*
>
> *- Hebrews 10:30-31*

> *For this is the will of God, your sanctification; that is, that you abstain from sexual immorality; that each of you know how to possess his own vessel in sanctification and honor, not in lustful passion, like the Gentiles who do not know God; and that no man transgress and defraud his brother in the matter because* **the Lord is the avenger in all these things, just as we also told you before and solemnly warned you.**
>
> *- 1 Thessalonians 4:3-6 (Emphasis added)*

Do not repay evil for evil but commit such people into the hands of God. Pray for mercy – if they have tremendously wronged you, fear for them. God will execute His wrath on them if they don't repent. Remember that it is a terrifying thing to fall into the hands of the living God, into the hands of an angry God.

> *Never pay back evil for evil to anyone. Respect what is right in the sight of all men. If possible, so far as it depends on you, be at peace with all men. Never take your own revenge, beloved, but leave room for the wrath of God, for it is written, "Vengeance is Mine, I will repay," says the Lord. "But if your enemy is hungry, feed him, and if he is thirsty, give him a drink; for in so doing you will heap burning coals on his head." Do not be overcome by evil, but overcome evil with good.*
>
> *- Romans 12:17-21*

Thus, this is the response the Bible offers for Christians to give in the face of such circumstances.

Interestingly David repented (*Psalm 51*), but his sins had extreme and dire consequences on his family (*2 Samuel 12:10-11*).

If you commit all these things into God's hands, He will take the burden of shame, depression and hurt from you, and you will feel His love, warmth and peace.

A sister at our church, whom I've known for years, experienced just this. She was a married woman with two children and a husband, who I believe was aspiring to become a church leader, and she was working as their administrator. In her life, things went rather severely indeed. In one week, her husband ran off with another married lady from the church, and the pastor of the church fired her from her job. In one week, as she later said, her life was utterly destroyed. She once said that she had contemplated suicide. God did for her what God always does – He drew near to her in her pain. During those troubled times, she drew near to God and prayed and spent time alone with Jesus up or three to four hours a day. She was able to walk away from what happened with her head held high and with peace and freedom – because God came in and healed her!

It is tough to deal with pain on that kind of level, but God does indeed draw near to people. He draws near to them in their suffering and actually becomes more real to them than He was before. He gives His peace, and that really is all people need to continue on the journey of life.

> *These things I have spoken to you, so that in Me you may have peace. In the world you have tribulation, but take courage; I have overcome the world."*
>
> *- John 16:33*

Suffering Due To Seemingly Random Circumstances

One thing that you can be sure of in life is that there will come a season of the suffering of what seems to be random pain. Life is a gift from God, but life has a way of dealing with terrible hands. There is even that terrible saying 'That's life'. So, what does this mean?

Only that seemingly random circumstances and painful situations do indeed take place. It is not always God's judgement or the devil's attacks.

> *Now on the same occasion there were some present who reported to Him about the Galileans whose blood Pilate had mixed with their sacrifices. And Jesus said to them, "Do you suppose that these Galileans were greater sinners than all other Galileans because they suffered this fate? I tell you, no, but unless you repent, you will all likewise perish. Or do you suppose that those eighteen on whom the tower in Siloam fell and killed them were worse culprits than all the men who live in Jerusalem? I tell you, no, but unless you repent, you will all likewise perish."*
>
> *- Luke 13:1-5*

Jesus is saying very clearly here that those Galileans did not suffer because they were greater sinners – but that in a fallen world, things sometimes go wrong, and it is nobody's fault. That may very well be life – but just to say, *'get over it because it's life,'* shows little to no sympathy!

> *And Jesus came up and spoke to them, saying, "All authority has been given to Me in heaven and on earth. Go therefore and make disciples of all the nations, baptizing them in the name of the Father and the Son and the Holy Spirit, teaching them to observe all that I commanded you; and lo, I am with you always, even to the end of the age."*
>
> *- Matthew 28:18-20*

You have to believe that Jesus has all authority – that is all authority over all things, including the things that happen to you in your life. In other words – there is nothing that happens in your life without His say so, not only that but He promises to always be with you even to the end of time itself!

So why then does God allow His people to pass through these tough situations? Think about one of the greatest Christians of all time – the Apostle Paul.[9]

> *For God, who said, "Light shall shine out of darkness," is the One*

> *who has shone in our hearts to give the Light of the knowledge of the glory of God in the face of Christ. But we have this treasure in earthen vessels, so that the surpassing greatness of the power will be of God and not from ourselves.*
>
> *- 2 Corinthians 4:6-7*

The Church is to be a light to a dying world. She has this treasure of Christ in mortal bodies and has the Answer to all of mankind's problems.

> *we are afflicted in every way, but not crushed; perplexed, but not despairing; persecuted, but not forsaken; struck down, but not destroyed.*
>
> *- 2 Corinthians 4:8-9*

Paul is describing the very tough circumstances that he had been through – and yet at the same time, he has not been destroyed by it all. God has kept him despite all the odds.

> *always carrying about in the body the dying of Jesus, so that the life of Jesus also may be manifested in our body. For we who live are constantly being delivered over to death for Jesus' sake, so that the life of Jesus also may be manifested in our mortal flesh.*
>
> *- 2 Corinthians 4:10-11*

Every Christian that God has the heart to use significantly has this process, which we can call being handed over to death. This is where God will allow a 'death situation' to work its way into the life of a Christian so that the life of Jesus Christ might be made manifest in the mortal body of the believer.

> *So death works in us, but life in you.*
>
> *- 2 Corinthians 4:12*

Paul was handed over to death so that life could be at work in the Corinthians and it's the same with you. God will allow bad things to happen to you so that the life of God will be able to flow out of you and minister life to those all around you. Remember that Jesus said you would have a river of life flowing out of you (*John 7:37-39*) which will water the lives of others. God has a heart for the world and is still seeking to save people. But the world is not looking for a Christian who's been untested and unproven. They are looking for the man or woman of God who has been tested and refined in purging fires, which have been through flood waters with faith that shines like gold! They want to see the man or woman who can testify to the whole world God's power to sustain the believer and transform who they are despite how difficult the circumstance or surroundings. Nobody likes suffering, but that's something that is going to happen until Jesus comes. You must not lose heart. There is a Saviour Who has suffered incredibly.

> *Therefore, since we have a great high priest who has passed through the heavens, Jesus the Son of God, let us hold fast our confession. For we do not have a high priest who cannot sympathize with our weaknesses, but One who has been tempted in all things as we are, yet without sin.*
>
> *- Hebrews 4:14-15*

To pray:

"Father, I am going through a lot of pain right now. I don't understand why this is happening to me, and I can't see the reason for it. But I know that You love me. I know and believe that my life is entirely in Your loving hands. Though I am going through great suffering, I know You will bring me through. I trust You, Lord, that You are in complete control. Please help me to see You and find You in every bad circumstance in my life. For all things work together for good to those who love You and have been called by You. In Jesus' Name. Amen."

CHAPTER THIRTEEN: SPIRITUAL DEPRESSION

Be of sober spirit, be on the alert. Your adversary, the devil, prowls around like a roaring lion, seeking someone to devour.

1 Peter 5:8

Not all depression is demonic. There can be many causes for it, including bereavement of a loved one, mental health issues, chemical imbalances in the body, stress from on-going hassles and pressures of life, etc. However, there is a depression that comes upon the Christian, which is spiritual in nature. This topic is written for a straightforward reason:

so that no advantage would be taken of us by Satan, for we are not ignorant of his schemes.

- 2 Corinthians 2:11

This is a war, and this world is a battleground. It must be remembered that living in this world is not the focus of the Church. Don't get too comfortable. It is not about living for today but rather living for tomorrow; the next world. The mission ordained is to preach the gospel and bring as many people to Heaven as possible. The enemy wants precisely the opposite. He wants to see as many people destroyed as he can. He operates in darkness, and God works in light (*John 1:5*); the devil operates in the world of sin. The more sin you have in your life, the more power you will allow him to have over you.

and do not give the devil an opportunity.
- Ephesians 4:27

Please remember that spiritual warfare is not a joke or a game. There is an enemy that is utterly ruthless and intends to destroy whomever he can. He will show no mercy. Christians, as part of God's army, have the power to drive demons out, not just out of people but out of homes too.

> **These signs will accompany those who have believed: in My name they will cast out demons**, *they will speak with new tongues; they will pick up serpents, and if they drink any deadly poison, it will not hurt them; they will lay hands on the sick, and they will recover."*
>
> *- Mark 16:17-18 (Emphasis added)*

Be careful. The power comes only from God. It is in His name that you drive out demons. Therefore to do such things, one has to be in Christ in the first place. Consider the following:

> *But also some of the Jewish exorcists, who went from place to place, attempted to name over those who had the evil spirits the name of the Lord Jesus, saying, "I adjure you by Jesus whom Paul preaches." Seven sons of one Sceva, a Jewish chief priest, were doing this. And the evil spirit answered and said to them, "I recognize Jesus, and I know about Paul, but who are you?" And the man, in whom was the evil spirit, leaped on them and subdued all*

of them and overpowered them, so that they fled out of that house naked and wounded.

- Acts 19:13-16

The demon recognised that these sons of Sceva had no authority over him. If you aren't in Christ, then you have no power over demons. The Bible tells of two kingdoms, one of light which is God's and one of darkness which is ruled over by the devil. If you are not in God's kingdom, then you are in the enemy's, and so consequently you are his subject. The power to drive out demons comes from God the Holy Spirit – remember that upon your conversion to Christ, the Spirit of God comes to live with you. He is the power source behind such things. Not you.

You are from God, little children, and have overcome them; because greater is He who is in you than he who is in the world.

- 1 John 4:4

So how does the enemy attack? One of the pieces of spiritual armour is the 'Shield of Faith' as described in Ephesians 6. The Shield is a defensive piece of equipment and is represented by faith. So what does it defend against? The flaming arrows of the evil one (*Ephesians 6:16*). The flaming arrows are discouragements and other like harassments that the enemy will throw at you to make you doubt God's character and to get you to give up the fight.

In the Garden of Eden, the devil came to Eve and challenged her belief regarding the faithfulness of God. He came to her with three words (*Genesis 3:1*)... 'Has God said?' Truth be told, you will hear those words all through your whole Christian life. It is all designed to take the eyes off of Jesus and onto oneself instead. His goal is to get the individual to doubt God – this is why faith is the defence. The Bible promises that if one resists the devil, then he will flee (James 4:7). So, therefore, he must be resisted. This is because the believer is washed in the blood of Jesus Christ (See 1 Corinthians 6:11 & Revelation 7:14), for there is power in the blood, and the forces of darkness find themselves with an impossible task. Therefore deception is their field of play, so to speak.

The problem for the believer is that the enemy will always try and come back, and all sin gives him a foothold. So deal with sin in your life and remain on guard against him if you want to overcome him. He is not an enemy that will give up.

What are the signs of someone coming under attack? These two general signs will show you if your depression is from demonic sources.

3. You will have a considerable irritation with Christian worship music.

4. You will have rage and anger directed towards God.

Worship to God is something the enemy can't stand. Why?

Yet You are holy,
O You who are enthroned upon the praises of Israel.
- Psalm 22:3

Where there is true worship, the Spirit of God will be there. Whether you are worshipping, or whether you have Christian music playing. Anywhere that God is satan can't stand, and he will attempt to drive out the music. You will, if you are under demonic oppression, get really offended and irritated by Christian music.

It must, however, be said that there is some Christian music that the devil doesn't seem to mind. Particularly if one cannot tell it is Christian! If the musicians are genuinely worshipping God, it is one thing. If however, it is just an act, or a show or even a concert then the enemy is not threatened by such music because the reality is that if God is not glorified by it but the flesh is then satan will not be bothered by it.

Now, satan and his demons have fury and rage against God.

> *For this reason, rejoice, O heavens and you who dwell in them. Woe to the earth and the sea, because the devil has come down to you, having great wrath, knowing that he has only a short time."*
>
> *- Revelation 12:12*

He knows he's on borrowed time. If the enemy puts his rage on you, you will find yourself getting mad at God.

> *So the dragon was enraged with the woman, and went off to make war with the rest of her children, who keep the commandments of God and hold to the testimony of Jesus.*
>
> *- Revelation 12:17*

Remember that there is a war going on, keep that in mind. Whether you like it or not if you commit your life to Jesus, you will have an enemy.

Why follow Jesus if the enemy is ready to pounce on His people?

> *When you were dead in your transgressions and the uncircumcision of your flesh, He made you alive together with Him, having forgiven us all our transgressions, having cancelled out the certificate of debt consisting of decrees against us, which was hostile to us; and He has taken it out of the way, having nailed it to the cross.* ***When He had disarmed the rulers and authorities, He made a public display of them, having triumphed over them through Him.***
>
> *- Colossians 2:13-15 (Emphasis added)*

The powers and authorities are fallen angels (also known as demons or evil and unclean spirits) – the unseen enemies of God. The cross of Jesus Christ has put satan into open shame and has defeated him. He is a most deadly foe nonetheless, but one that has been defeated. His only weapon more or less is his mouth. To speak doubts, fears or even threats into your life. Of course, he is also the power force behind the world, and there are always people willing to do his bidding. Generally, his attacks will target your mind.

Your depression could be demonic, but it must be noted that demonic possession is different from an attack. Being possessed is when you have demons inside you. You get attacked from outside of you. This is similar to what the Apostle Paul experienced with his thorn (*See 2 Corinthians 12:7-9*).

This is not just to harass you but also to bring division in your family and stop the work of God.

> *If a house is divided against itself, that house will not be able to stand.*
>
> *- Mark 3:25*

It is so important to have discernment and wisdom because satan will work all kinds of tricks and deceits against you. He knows your weaknesses and how to push your buttons. So you must guard against him.

You fight him with the Sword of the Spirit. This weapon is referred to as the Word of God, and it is an offensive weapon.

> *For the word of God is living and active and sharper than any two-edged sword, and piercing as far as the division of soul and spirit, of both joints and marrow, and able to judge the thoughts and intentions of the heart.*
>
> *- Hebrews 4:12*

How do you use the Word of God as your weapon? You remind satan what God has said and what God is still saying! This is why it is so important to regularly read the Bible. How can you use God's promises to attack the devil when you don't know them?

The answer is straightforward. You cannot.

It is also worth noting that Jesus is called by the Apostle John the 'Word of God.' As if everything God speaks, every promise He has made and everything He has declared is climaxed and entirely fulfilled in the Lord Jesus Christ. Now here is what the Bible says about that spiritual armour:

> *For our struggle is not against flesh and blood, but against the rulers, against the powers, against the world forces of this darkness, against the spiritual forces of wickedness in the heavenly places. Therefore, take up the full armor of God, so that you will be able to resist in the evil day, and having done everything, to stand firm. Stand firm therefore, having girded your loins with truth, and having put on the breastplate of righteousness, and having shod your feet with the preparation of the gospel of peace; in addition to all, taking up the shield of faith with which you will be able to extinguish all the flaming arrows of the evil one. And take the helmet of salvation, and the sword of the Spirit, which is the word of God.*
>
> *- Ephesians 6:12-17*

1. Helmet of Salvation – The helmet is the most crucial piece of armour. It protects the head, which is where the brain is. Salvation is the most essential part of the fighting. You can't fight the enemy if you are his subject in his kingdom. This is also called the hope of salvation (*see 1 Thessalonians 5:8*)

2. Breastplate of Righteousness – The breastplate covers most of our vital organs. You must, as the Bible says to put on the Lord Jesus (*Romans 13:14*), remember that the cross gives you His righteousness. Hence His name The-LORD-Is-Our-Righteousness (*Jeremiah 33:16*). This is also called the breastplate of faith and love (*see 1 Thessalonians 5:8*).

3. Belt of Truth – The belt holds the whole armour together. You **must** be grounded in truth. Truth is anything that corresponds to what the Bible says. Error is anything that contradicts it. All divine truth must be in line with the Bible, 100%.

4. Feet shod with the preparation of the gospel of peace – You must be ready to share the gospel in or out of season (*2 Tim-*

othy 4:2), be prepared with all readiness when the occasion presents itself.

5. Sword of the Spirit – This is the Word of God. You attack with God's Word, but our main attack is in the form of prayer. You pray against the enemy, and you pray for people. When you pray to God, and you quote from the Bible whether you are praying for someone or praying against the enemy, it is a powerful prayer. It should be noted that private prayer comes before public prayer.

6. Shield of Faith – You remind yourself of the promises and the faithfulness of God. Your faith in God is your defence.

It is worth noting that for the Roman soldier's uniform, there is no protection on the back. This is to discourage soldiers from fleeing from battle. The armour of the Christian is the same; Christians are not to turn their backs to the enemy.

> *But Jesus said to him, "No one, after putting his hand to the plow and looking back, is fit for the kingdom of God."*
>
> *- Luke 9:62*

A shocking word from the Lord, but why fight? Think of your loved ones, think of your friends and those you know who are all bound by satan and led captive to do his will (*2 Timothy 2:26*).

> *When I saw their fear, I rose and spoke to the nobles, the officials and the rest of the people: "Do not be afraid of them; remember the Lord who is great and awesome, and fight for your brothers, your sons, your daughters, your wives and your houses."*
>
> *- Nehemiah 4:14*

This is not about you and the devil; this is much bigger than that. You are fighting for your family. You are fighting for your siblings. You are fighting for your parents. You are fighting for your children. You are fighting for your friends.

In the book of 1 Samuel, Israel had an ancient enemy called the Philistines – a picture of us and the devil with his demon powers and principalities. One day, Jonathan decides to go and fight the Philistines in one of their garrisons, with his loyal armour bearer joining him.

> *Then Jonathan climbed up on his hands and feet, with his armor bearer behind him; and they fell before Jonathan, and his armor bearer put some to death after him. That first slaughter which Jonathan and his armor bearer made was about twenty men within about half a furrow in an acre of land.*
>
> *- 1 Samuel 14:13-14*

Notice three things. Firstly, that to get to the victory, Jonathan had to be on his hands and knees – similarly, you must be on your hands and knees seeking God if you are going to win the fight! Secondly, he fought only on a piece of ground about half an acre in size – you may not have much to fight for, but you need to defend what little God has given you. Finally, Jonathan had a faithful companion to fight with him by his side – you also will have a loyal companion to fight with you; the Lord Jesus Christ.

So whatever it takes, you fight for those you love – you never know how many lives might be changed, all because you decided to fight when those around you were giving up all hope.

To pray:

> *"Father, I want to fight as You would have me. Help me today as I put on my Helmet of Salvation, Breastplate of Righteousness, Belt of Truth, Feet shod with the preparation of the gospel of peace, Sword of the Spirit and the Shield of Faith. I take my stand against satan, and I declare in the Name of Jesus that I will resist him. I will not allow him to steal from me, to kill or destroy in my life or the lives of those I love.*
>
> *satan in the Name of the Lord Jesus Christ, I resist you and your lies. Go away from me and those I love. I command it in Jesus' Name. Amen."*

CHAPTER FOURTEEN: WHEN GOD HIDES HIS FACE

*You hide Your face, they are dismayed;
You take away their spirit, they
expire and return to their dust.*

Psalm 104:29

There are many reasons why God chooses to hide. It may well be due to sin, it could be due to other voices coming in and overcrowding His voice, hardening of hearts, etc. Still, there is explicitly a time of God's hiding. A time (many times even) will come when God will withdraw from you. You won't know whether He's there or not.

Remember, in the book of Job, that Job was a righteous man who God even commended to satan. Due to a few conversations that God had with satan, Job lost everything! What was worse for Job was that God seemed not to take any notice. He seemed not to be anywhere in sight.

"Why do You hide Your face

And consider me Your enemy?
- Job 13:24

Christians can often feel like Job – when God withdraws His presence, the temptation is to get hurt and assume that God is mad for some hidden sin. Not always so! There is a passage from Isaiah that shall be expanded so you can understand why maybe God seems to have hidden from you, and you have examined your heart honestly and can find no sin. The passage concerned is Isaiah 45:15-19.

Truly, You are a God who hides Himself,
O God of Israel, Savior!
They will be put to shame and even humiliated, all of them;
The manufacturers of idols will go away together in humiliation.

- Isaiah 45:15-16

God does hide from time to time. It is clear that there are those who do not trust in the Lord. God is making it clear that those who make idols will be brought to shame – so what about those who believe in the Lord?

Israel has been saved by the Lord
With an everlasting salvation;
You will not be put to shame or humiliated
To all eternity.

- Isaiah 45:17

Those who trust in the Lord will be saved! That is whether or not you can feel His presence at this precise moment in time. If you have Christ, then you have life! Stop relying on your feelings! Rise above your feelings.

For thus says the Lord, who created the heavens (He is the God who formed the earth and made it, He established it and did not create it a waste place, but formed it to be inhabited),

"I am the Lord, and there is none else.
"I have not spoken in secret,
In some dark land;
I did not say to the offspring of Jacob,
'Seek Me in a waste place';
I, the Lord, speak righteousness,
Declaring things that are upright.

- Isaiah 45:18-19

As God created the earth to be inhabited, so He hides to be sought. The one thing God wants from His people is that they would look for Him. One of the reasons God hides is because He wants people to seek Him, with all their heart, soul, mind and strength.

Consider the story of Elisha and the Shunammite woman in 2 Kings 4. Elisha came to her, and God blessed her with a son. One day Elisha goes off on a long journey. Meanwhile, as Elisha is journeying, this woman's son dies. She then, without telling anyone, immediately sets off in search of Elisha. The most remarkable thing about this whole story is that when she greeted Elisha, he, being the prophet of God, didn't have a clue why she'd come. He greeted her as usual unaware that her son had just died!

When she came to the man of God to the hill, she caught hold of his feet. And Gehazi came near to push her away; but the man of God said, "Let her alone, for her soul is troubled within her; and **the Lord has hidden it from me and has not told me."**

- 2 Kings 4:27 (Emphasis added)

Why did God hide this woman's pain from Elisha? Was God indifferent? Was God showing a lack of concern for this woman's problem? **Not at all**. If you read carefully, you'll see that God is trying to say something very profound here. Elisha was the prophet of God and, in those days, the prophet was the spokesperson for God. If God had told Elisha the problem, he would have gone to her and 'sorted' the issue out. There's a more profound work going on here that you may realise.

God hid from this woman so that she would seek Him! True, she ran to the prophet, but she was in a way running to God. If Elisha had just come to her and healed her boy, then she would not have sought after Elisha and consequently God. You must **never** take His presence for granted.

But another reason that God hides is to test people, to see if they will cling to Him; if they will chase after Him. God wants to know if they miss Him when He's not (apparently) there.

> *Even in the matter of the envoys of the rulers of Babylon, who sent to him to inquire of the wonder that had happened in the land,* ***God left him alone only to test him, that He might know all that was in his heart****.*
>
> *- 2 Chronicles 32:31 (Emphasis added)*

God will test us to see if our hearts are open to Him, to know if we really are pressing hard towards Him. God withdrew from Hezekiah to see if his heart was pure towards Him. God will do the same to us.

> *You shall follow the Lord your God and fear Him; and you shall keep His commandments, listen to His voice, serve Him, and cling to Him.*
>
> *- Deuteronomy 13:4*

God wants us to cling to Him. It is only when we earnestly seek Him that He is found by us. One of the most frightening passages of the whole Bible can be found in Judges 16. Samson was a man that was much used by God. However, if you read the book of Judges, you will see that Samson was a man that despised the ways of God. He was eventually tricked by Delilah into giving her, the secret to his great strength.

> *She said, "The Philistines are upon you, Samson!" And he awoke from his sleep and said, "I will go out as at other times and shake*

myself free." **But he did not know that the Lord had departed from him.**

- Judges 16:20 (Emphasis added)

What an awful thing happened to the heart of Samson. God completely lifted His presence, and the most terrible thing is that Samson did not even notice that God had left.

God withdraws from His people because He knows that if they don't go through these desert experiences, then there is a great temptation to neglect the presence of God and to end up totally blinded and under the enemy's power grinding grain in his house as Samson did. A defeated man!

Then the Philistines seized him and gouged out his eyes; and they brought him down to Gaza and bound him with bronze chains, and he was a grinder in the prison.

- Judges 16:21

The more time you spend with the Lord, the more you become aware of His sweet presence. You will know when He is near, and you will also recognise when He leaves.

Sadly, I have been to churches where the Holy Spirit was completely absent from the worship, but none of the worshippers noticed it. The problem is that people often confuse the hype and emotions of the moment for God's Spirit. They do not realise that God may not actually be among them as they think.

If the Holy Spirit really is moving, lives will change and become more holy. If you come away from a meeting very happy, but you remain the same in your sins, then this should greatly alarm you. God is not always in the meeting, even if everybody's having a good time. Also, just because you shed some tears at church doesn't mean that it is the Holy Spirit – He does do this, and yes, there are tears as a result. Yet you must understand that emotions can greatly deceive. If you judge your Christian life based on the feelings you feel in the heat of a meeting, then the chances are that you are not judging accurately.

> *"This is another thing you do: you cover the altar of the Lord with tears, with weeping and with groaning, because He no longer regards the offering or accepts it with favor from your hand. Yet you say, 'For what reason?' Because the Lord has been a witness between you and the wife of your youth, against whom you have dealt treacherously, though she is your companion and your wife by covenant.*
>
> *- Malachi 2:13-14*

God is saying that these people cover His altar with their tears but then go out and cheat on their wives. Some Christians think they can cry and cry and cry – and because they do that, then they can go out and do what they please.

I know of a sister who attended a church. Every time she was there, a sensation would come over her to break down and weep. Every other Christian was rejoicing in God and having a good time worshipping. Later it was revealed that the pastor was cheating on his wife with a married woman in the church.

It was a whole church full of Christians, and only one of them was connected to the broken heart of Jesus. Thirty minutes of singing a week are not enough to know His heart. That's why He hides – to spur one on to seek after Him more.

Remember the Bible says that the Holy Spirit is with you (*1 John 14:17*) and is even within you if you are a Christian. Jesus Himself promised that He would always be with His people (*Matthew 28:20*) and would never leave or forsake them (*Hebrews 13:5*).

> *Now before the Feast of the Passover, Jesus knowing that His hour had come that He would depart out of this world to the Father,* **having loved His own who were in the world, He loved them to the end.**
>
> *- John 13:1 (Emphasis added)*

This is a promise, regardless of your feelings. If you feel God has distanced Himself from you and you can't perceive anything in you that would offend Him then don't worry. Keep seeking Him, and He will allow you to find Him. You must not give up.

You will seek Me and find Me when you search for Me with all your heart.

- Jeremiah 29:13

O Lord, by Your favor You have made my mountain to stand strong;
You hid Your face, I was dismayed.
To You, O Lord, I called,
And to the Lord I made supplication:
"What profit is there in my blood, if I go down to the pit?
Will the dust praise You? Will it declare Your faithfulness?

"Hear, O Lord, and be gracious to me;
O Lord, be my helper."
You have turned for me my mourning into dancing;
You have loosed my sackcloth and girded me with gladness,
That my soul may sing praise to You and not be silent.
O Lord my God, I will give thanks to You forever.

- Psalm 30:7-12

To pray:

"Father, thank You very much that You take our relationship with You very seriously. If You are so committed to preserving it and making sure it is authentic, then I will do my part in seeking You. Even though I can feel alone many times, I know that I am not alone because You are always with me. Thank You so much for this friendship. May this be the most important thing in my life. In Jesus' Name. Amen."

CHAPTER FIFTEEN: THE INTELLECTUAL'S BARRIER

Where is the wise man? Where is the scribe? Where is the debater of this age? Has not God made foolish the wisdom of the world?

1 Corinthians 1:20

There is a problem that has caused many to stumble in the faith and to turn away from walking with Jesus.

For the word of the cross is foolishness to those who are perishing, but to us who are being saved it is the power of God. For it is written, "I will destroy the wisdom of the wise, and the cleverness of the clever I will set aside."

- 1 Corinthians 1:18-19

The problem can be called 'the intellectual's barrier'. Intellectuals have a problem because the cross of Jesus Christ is the only way for salvation. They can't think, imagine or even philosophise their way into the Kingdom. It's an offence because their good works count for nothing. They are insulted with the suggestion that eternal life is so simple – just look and live.

> *Truly I say to you, whoever does not receive the kingdom of God like a child will not enter it at all."*
>
> *- Mark 10:15*

What does Jesus mean by that? Quite simply, all that is required for someone to come to God is childlike faith. Parents can persuade their little children to believe whatever they tell them. It's perfect simplicity. But many intellectual people try to work everything out for themselves only to trip over themselves!

> *But I am afraid that, as the serpent deceived Eve by his craftiness, your minds will be led astray from the simplicity and purity of devotion to Christ.*
>
> *- 2 Corinthians 11:3*

God created minds, God gave people the ability to reason, but what many of these sincere but mistaken people are doing, by reason, logic and science, is to try and work out God, to try and work out the Bible. You cannot do that to the things of God for Science, logic and reason belong to the natural realm, not the supernatural realm. You cannot convince natural men of God's existence by the use of reason and science.

> *But a natural man does not accept the things of the Spirit of God, for they are foolishness to him; and he cannot understand them, because they are spiritually appraised.*
>
> *- 1 Corinthians 2:14*

Some people demand a visible, tangible sign before they will believe. The Pharisees asked Jesus for the same thing – and His response to them is the same as it is to such men today:

> *An evil and adulterous generation seeks after a sign; and a sign will not be given it, except the sign of Jonah." And He left them*

and went away.

- Matthew 16:4

God won't jump to the whimsies of any man. God bypasses the smart people who think so highly of themselves.

For consider your calling, brethren, that there were not many wise according to the flesh, not many mighty, not many noble; but God has chosen the foolish things of the world to shame the wise, and God has chosen the weak things of the world to shame the things which are strong, and the base things of the world and the despised God has chosen, the things that are not, so that He may nullify the things that are, so that no man may boast before God.

- 1 Corinthians 1:26-29

People need to stop. They won't find God in the realm of nature, that is, in the natural way of doing things. God's creation does point to His power as Creator, but it can only do just that; point. It cannot take you directly to Him, and many people are missing it for they are missing God by being so natural. So the question remains...how do you find God?

At that time Jesus said, "I praise You, Father, Lord of heaven and earth, that You have hidden these things from the wise and intelligent and have revealed them to infants. Yes, Father, for this way was well-pleasing in Your sight.

- Matthew 11:25-26

You come to God on His terms, not yours and God has clearly declared that it is for people to come to Him humbly as little children with faith. By all means, you ought to think and not throw your brains out. Yet you need to remember that it is by a childlike faith that you need to come to God. You cannot understand God. Instead, you can seek Him. That is all that is required to find Him. God is not obliged to do anything to prove Himself to anyone. If you want access to God, you must come by the route of faith through Jesus Christ. Otherwise, you will not find Him.

And without faith it is impossible to please Him, for he who comes to God must believe that He is and that He is a rewarder of those who seek Him.

- Hebrews 11:6

To pray:

"Father, I am sorry for trying to understand You with my mind. I confess that I have found it difficult to approach You because of logic and reason. Yet I know that I will have all the evidence I need if I will simply come in faith and give You all my life. I trust You, Lord, even if I don't understand it all. Give me the faith I need to approach You in the right way. In Jesus' Name. Amen."

REFERENCES

Epigraph - retrieved from: https://www.azquotes.com/quote/863763

[1]Taken with permission: https://www.youngwriterssociety.com/work/Gravity/Where-is-God-When-I-Need-Him-108447
https://www.youngwriterssociety.com/work/Gravity/memberlist.php?mode=viewprofile&u=36754&sid=ffaac22537a43c213f629a8275e9f590

[2]https://www.dictionary.com/browse/cultivate

[3]Taken with permission from Tozer on the Almighty God: A 365-Day Devotion, compiled by Ron Eggert, ©2004 by Moody Bible Institute of Chicago authored by A. W. Tozer.

[4]https://www.dictionary.com/browse/reconciliation?s=t

[5]Taken with permission from ©2005, 2009 by Moody Bible Institute of Chicago, authored by A. W. Tozer

[6]Strong's Exhaustive Concordance of the Bible by James Strong, copyright 2007 by Hendrickson Publishers, Peabody, Massachusetts. Used by permission. All rights reserved.

[7]Ibid.

[8]Taken with permission from World Challenge Pulpit Series, Roving Eyes by David Wilkerson, November 28, 1988

[9]Some ideas from this chapter are taken from sermons by David Wilkerson: The Ever Increasing Demands of Faith (July 20, 2008) & Handed Over to Death (January 10, 1999). http://tsc.nyc/media_center.php?pg=sermons&mi=1065 & http://tsc.nyc/media_center.php?pg=sermons&mi=21832, re-

spectively.

Printed in Poland
by Amazon Fulfillment
Poland Sp. z o.o., Wrocław